W9-AFJ-310

BE
A
PLAYER

BE
A
PLAYER

A BREAKTHROUGH
APPROACH TO PLAYING BETTER
ON THE GOLF COURSE

Pia Nilsson & Lynn Marriott

WITH SUSAN K. REED

ATRIA BOOKS

New York London Toronto Sydney New Delhi

ATRIA
B O O K S

An Imprint of Simon & Schuster, Inc.
1230 Avenue of the Americas
New York, NY 10020

First Atria Books hardcover edition June 2017

ATRIA B O O K S and colophon are trademarks of Simon & Schuster, Inc.

For information about special discounts for bulk purchases,
please contact Simon & Schuster Special Sales at 1-866-506-1949
or business@simonandschuster.com.

The Simon & Schuster Speakers Bureau can bring authors
to your live event. For more information or to book an event,
contact the Simon & Schuster Speakers Bureau at 1-866-248-3049
or visit our website at www.simonspeakers.com.

Interior design by Tim Oliver

Manufactured in the United States of America

10 9 8 7 6 5 4 3 2 1

Library of Congress Cataloging-in-Publication Data

Names: Nilsson, Pia, author. | Marriott, Lynn, author. | Reed, Susan K., author.
Title: Be a player : a breakthrough approach to playing better on the golf course /
    By Pia Nilsson and Lynn Marriott ; With Susan K. Reed.
Description: First Atria Books hardcover edition. | New York : Atria Books, 2017.
Identifiers: LCCN 2016057505| ISBN 9781476788036 (hardback) |
    ISBN 9781476788043 (ebook)
Subjects: LCSH: Golf—Training. | Golf—Psychological aspects. | BISAC: SPORTS
    & RECREATION / Golf. | SPORTS & RECREATION / Sports Psychology. |
    SPORTS & RECREATION / Coaching / General.
Classification: LCC GV979.T68 N54 2017 | DDC 796.352—dc23 LC record available at
    https://lccn.loc.gov/2016057505

ISBN 978-1-4767-8803-6
ISBN 978-1-4767-8804-3 (ebook)

*We dedicate this book to the people
who have influenced us and shaped our view
of the game and of human potential.
We recognize a few of them in these pages,
but there are many, many others.
We stand on their shoulders, and are forever
grateful for their wisdom and support.*

*We dedicate this book
to the Supergolfer in each of us.
Let us keep believing in our futures—
and bringing our possibilities to life.*

CONTENTS

DURING THE ROUND
BETWEEN SHOTS—YOUR BODY, MIND, AND EMOTIONS

BEFORE, DURING, AND AFTER THE ROUND
YOUR HUMAN INVENTORY

INTRODUCTION:
A NEW WAY TO IMPROVE

NEARLY EVERY WEEK, a new group of golfers arrives for one of our VISION54 programs at Talking Stick Golf Club in Scottsdale, Arizona. The students include top amateurs, aspiring tour players, and recreational golfers—among them lawyers, filmmakers, bankers, opera singers, corporate executives, and teachers. All of them love golf. All of them want to improve and enjoy the game. But more often than not, they admit to being frustrated with golf—and with themselves. Sadly, some are just about ready to quit.

Listen to a few of our students. We always begin by asking them to introduce themselves and to say a few words about why they've come.

Janice, from Vancouver, British Columbia: "I love golf when I play well, but I really struggle when I'm playing poorly. I wonder if it's possible to have fun even when I'm having a bad day."

Joe, from Minneapolis, Minnesota: "I feel frustrated most of the time I'm on the course. I'd like to learn how to be more relaxed and spend less time thinking about the mechanics of my swing."

Beth, from Boston, Massachusetts, a retired finance executive: "I'm very analytical and goal-oriented. I want to get out of my head and feel more joy when I play."

Mia, from Pittsburgh, Pennsylvania, who is a college golfer: "The biggest thing I'm looking for is to improve my consistency. After rounds when I played well I think, *That was so easy.* But after a bad round I'm thinking, *That was the hardest thing I've ever done.*"

Bob, from Portland, Oregon: "My main objective and desire is to get the most out of myself. I want to feel I can improve and continue to grow my golf game."

Lana, who lives in Lake Tahoe, Nevada, and Palm Desert, California: "I love golf, but I never feel like I'm improving. And I fight the feeling that not improving reflects on me as a person."

Mike, from Scottsdale, Arizona, a businessman: "I want to be able to manage myself better when I play with my weekend foursome. They talk so much: I can't even concentrate. I play like Jekyll and Hyde when I'm with them."

Ida, from Kansas City, Missouri: "I so want to enjoy golf. When I don't play well, I beat myself up and have a terrible rest of the day."

Zach, from New York City, a 1-handicap player: "Instead of always thinking about my swing, I want to learn to let myself play the game."

Julie, from Indiana, a nationally ranked amateur: "I don't want to be so scared when I'm playing."

Jane, from New York: "I want to figure out why I get so tight when I'm hitting over water. I moan and groan a lot on the course. I don't want to be that kind of golfer."

Patrick, from New Jersey, who works in venture capital: "I practice and take lessons, but I never seem to get any better. Most days, I come off the course completely deflated. I don't want to start all over. I'd like to take my game—the one I have now—to the next level."

The sentiments of the comments capture the mood we see in today's golfers—whether they are American, European, or

Asian. Though club technology, fitness training, and the science of the swing have improved exponentially over the past decade, many golfers have not improved and have been leaving the game. The numbers have declined for several reasons, from a shortage of playing time and budget considerations, to difficulty in learning the game and courses that are too challenging. In short, golfers are stuck—and their lack of improvement might be a more alarming development for the game. According to the National Golf Foundation, nearly six million people in the U.S. quit the sport between 2003 and 2015.

We think we know another big reason why players are frustrated. Many golfers struggle to transfer their games from the range to the course. We see players making good contact in practice, but when we're watching them on the course, they take three times longer to hit the ball—with a completely different technical swing. All of a sudden, they can't hit the ball. Their physical, mental, and emotional states have changed because performing on the golf course *means something*. There are actual consequences to what they do.

Consider this: What if you arrive at a tennis court or a basketball court and see a sign that reads: NO PRACTICING ON THE COURT. Or at a swimming pool, the lifeguard tells you, "Sorry, no practicing your breast stroke in the pool." Many golf courses and clubs have similar rules, ostensibly to protect pace of play and the conditions of the course.

Here's what we believe: Practicing golf shots and playing golf on the course are not incompatible. To learn a sport, you need to learn *in the context of the sport with all its constraints.* Only in this state can you learn the skills that are required *in the real environment of the game.*

In addition to teaching the mechanics of a pitch shot on the range, golfers need to learn to hit that shot on the course, and then how to hit it a little higher to get over a bunker or a bush (and with only one try!). Let's say there's a tree in front of you. You need to get the ball around the tree. The first time you try, you'll probably stick the ball in the trunk of the tree. But with exploration and practice, you'll figure out how to navigate around the tree. All of a sudden, you've learned to curve the ball. You've learned to *play*.

The bottom line is that you have to be in the pool to learn how to swim, you have to be on a tennis court to learn to play tennis, and you have to be on the golf course to learn the game. You need to dedicate time on the course when you're not focused on keeping score. You need to be on the course to discover what works. (And we promise, doing so will not hold up play or leave hundreds of divots.) Only on the course will you truly develop your skills, your game—and yourself.

A related issue we've observed is that when golfers (of any level) struggle on the course, they tend to blame their technique. Players today have become entirely too focused on the swing, with its angles and planes, speeds and smash factors. Tour pros now spend hours analyzing their swings with video cameras and TrackMan-style launch-monitor devices. (These instruments measure everything from clubhead speed to ball speed and flight apex to the forces and pressures of the feet during the swing.) Amateur golfers are convinced they'll shoot lower scores once they've figured out whether they're one-plane or two-plane swingers. They debate swing theories—X-factor, Stack-and-Tilt, A-Swing—as if one is the right answer. They read magazine articles that promise to teach the correct swing method that will fix everything. Meanwhile, they pursue the elusive secret of the swing via instructional apps and the wide array of analytical resources, such as K-VESTs, FocusBands, and clip-on metronomes. As one of our students put it, "I've taken in so much information, I feel like my head is exploding."

We want to make it clear that we're not dismissing the benefit of modern technology or the importance of a sound golf swing. It's imperative that you have a reliable swing that fits your body. You need to practice it enough, so you are confident and can execute it proficiently. You also need to know which situations call for a certain shot. Even so, we believe there's an important distinction. It's not just about the swing. *It's about the golfer who makes the swing on the course.*

There's a book we like called *The Dude and the Zen Master.* It's a series of conversations between the actor Jeff Bridges and a Zen master named Bernie Glassman. Glassman was an aeronautical engineer who became a teacher of Buddhism in Los Angeles. In the book, Bernie and Jeff discuss a variety of subjects, from movies to family to learning to, well, simply, being human. Bernie tells Jeff that he knows a little ditty that contains one of the secrets to life:

Row, row, row your boat,
Gently down the stream,
Merrily, merrily, merrily, merrily,
Life is but a dream.

He asks Jeff to imagine getting into a boat for the first time and trying to figure out how to row. Should he put the right oar into the water first or the left? What should he be doing with his shoulders during the stroke? What about his arms? How can he get the oars to work together? What if he wants to row to the opposite shore? If he fixates on the destination, he might forget to pay attention to his rowing mechanics. But if he fixates on his rowing, he could lose focus on where he wants to go.

Bernie explains that, according to Zen philosophy, the opposite shore is actually right under your feet. So the question isn't, *How do you get from here to there?* The question is, *How do you get from here to here?* How do you become fully present in the moment, in your environment, and in the activity in which you're engaged?

Bernie advises Jeff, "Don't get down on yourself because you're not an expert rower right away. Don't go learn to row in a performance tank. Just ease your boat into the water and begin to row—very gently—down the stream."

IN OUR PREVIOUS BOOKS, *Every Shot Must Have a Purpose, The Game Before the Game,* and *Play Your Best Golf Now,* we introduced the elements of our teaching: Shot-making with purpose and commitment, practice that reflects the real game, and skills that enable you to access physical, mental, and emotional states that lead to better play. But we believe the place you can really improve your game is on the golf course, so in this book, we'll teach you what we call "human skills," which you'll rely on in the actual context of the game. As you learn these skills, you will learn more about yourself. You will be able to rely on yourself. You will be able to adjust. You will become your own best coach. Which means, you'll be a player.

In our opinion, there are four pillars that support a golfer's game: 1) your fitness level, 2) your technical skills (that is, your swing and stroke), 3) your equipment, and 4) your human skills. Unfortunately, the human skills are rarely taught—and to us, these are essential to playing good golf.

We look at it this way: Once you step onto the golf course, can you change your fitness level, your technical skills, or your equipment? No. The only one of these pillars you have control over on the course is your human skills. Developing these skills—especially self-awareness and self-management—will help you play your best. Human skills will also help you manage emotions that invariably arise on the course, such as anxiety, frustration, fear, discouragement, and anger. They can also help you create positive states such as focus, confidence, equanimity, courage, and joy—all of which help you enjoy the game more.

During our collective 64 years of teaching and coaching, we've become super-interested in the conditions that facilitate peak performance—that is, when people are performing at the highest level of their abilities. Whether the performers are dancers, musicians, surgeons, or golfers, one common denominator is that, in the moment of performance, they are fully present through their senses—particularly sight, sound, and feel. When this happens, we are capable of far more than we've ever imagined.

It's why we named our company VISION54. We wanted to invoke a new frontier, the idea that a golfer will shoot a score of 54 someday. That could mean making birdies on all 18 holes, or a combination of pars, birdies, and eagles. 54 is a number. It's also a philosophy oriented toward possibilities rather than limitations. 54 is a process of changing old habits and learning new ones. It's a discipline of managing your physical, mental, and emotional states on a golf course—in an environment that's always changing.

We have full confidence that a golfer will shoot 54 someday soon: To date, fewer than 20 players have carded a 59 in competition. One of the 59-shooters, Annika Sorenstam, was coached by Pia. Another, Russell Knox, is a PGA Tour professional we currently coach. (By the way, we append the number 54 to the names of all players we coach: Russell Knox is "Roo54." He gets his nickname, Roo, because he carries a kangaroo headcover. PGA Tour winner Kevin Streelman is "Streels54," and another of our students, Condoleezza Rice, is "Condi54.") So, what will it take to open the door to the next performance breakthrough in golf? In our opinion, shooting 54 will require a paradigm shift from a "faults-and-fixes" approach to a "possibilities-and-excellence" approach that will additionally rely on human skills.

We think of this as a back-to-the-future concept. When the Society of St. Andrews Golfers was founded in 1754, there were no professional instructors, no practice ranges, and no swing simulators. Golfers learned to play on the course, in the context of the game. They figured out how to properly flight a shot, manage their nerves, and focus on the parts of the game they could control. Throughout history, great champions have embodied these skills: Old Tom Morris, Joyce Wethered, Bobby Jones, Ben Hogan, Kathy Whitworth, Arnold Palmer, Nancy Lopez, Jack Nicklaus, Tiger Woods, and Annika Sorenstam used their *human skills* to become *great players* of the game. It's our opinion that these skills don't have to remain implicit, or mysterious, or the province of champions. Today, thanks to advances in science and performance research, and our years of observing and coaching golfers, we can help make implicit skills explicit.

In the following chapters, you'll learn these human skills

on the course alongside some of our professional and amateur students: current and former LPGA Tour players Suzann Pettersen, Brittany Lang, Ariya Jutanugarn, and Annika Sorenstam; current and former PGA Tour players Russell Knox, Kevin Streelman, and Arron Oberholser; amateurs such as Condoleezza Rice and A.K. Frazier and Amy Lane, to name a few. These players acquired human skills that enabled them to *play to their full potential.*

Recent research in fields such as psychophysiology, neuroscience, and athletic training have changed the way we think about how we learn, what our true capacities are, and what creates peak performance. These fields incorporate medicine, psychology, physiology, brain science, nutrition, biofeedback, contextual learning, and meditation. They propose that we have a capacity to learn and perform at a higher level than most had ever imagined, enabling us to bridge the long-assumed mind/body divide. This allows us to consider golf in a new light, because it points directly to us; we are capable of more improvement, growth, and self-regulation than we thought possible. However, the *work* of crossing this mind/body divide, and attaining these larger goals, is up to each of us.

We're not alone in discovering a new, forward-thinking philosophy. Many of our peers in golf and other sports are just as committed to these new ideas. In this book, we want to introduce some of the people and concepts that have influenced us over the years—innovative teachers like Chuck Hogan and Kjell Enhager; human-potential thinkers such as Michael Murphy and Ken Wilber; scientists and psychologists the likes of JoAnne Whitaker and Carol Dweck; techniques like Heart-Math, and even an approach to communication and personal growth called Neuro-Linguistic Programming. We've studied these disciplines, extracted the best ideas, and incorporated them into our VISION54 methodology. In doing so, we have discovered that bringing higher awareness to our bodies, minds, and emotions can release our true potential.

This journey will be interior (you, the human being) and exterior (you on the golf course). Our goal is to introduce you to the human skills *in context,* and help you understand how to use them. Each chapter includes Questions and On-Course Explorations. The explorations should always be done *on the course.* The purpose is to spur you to reflect and become more aware, so you can discover what makes you play your best. We want you to blend the explorations into your rounds—the more you use them, the more natural and organic they'll become. And the more they'll change your game. We hope you'll engage them with three words we cherish: *awareness, intention,* and *attention.* Instead of beating balls to death on the range, we hope you'll make these human skills the heart of your game.

Come with us. Let's explore golf in a whole new way.

BEFORE
THE
ROUND
YOUR FOUNDATIONAL HUMAN SKILLS

CHAPTER 1

AWARENESS: ALL LEARNING STARTS HERE

I
N DECEMBER 2006, Norwegian golfer Suzann Pettersen signed up for one of our VISION54 programs in Arizona. Suzann is undoubtedly one of the most gifted athletes in sports today. She grew up skiing and had a storied junior golf career, winning the Norwegian Amateur Championship five times and the British Girls Championship once. As a teenager, she represented Norway in the World Amateur Team Championship and was selected for the Junior European Ryder Cup. Suzann turned pro in 2000 at 19 years old; the following year she finished second on the Ladies European Tour Order of Merit and was named LET Rookie of the Year. In 2003, Suzann qualified for the LPGA Tour. To many of us who knew her, she was headed for guaranteed stardom. But over the next six years, despite a handful of top-10 finishes on the LPGA Tour and several brilliant Solheim Cup appearances, Suzann never won a professional tournament.

She was 25 years old when she arrived for our three-day school. She looked glum and told us she was frustrated and depressed about her game.

Pia said to her, "Suzann, I've watched you since you were a junior, and you're one of the most talented players I've ever seen. When you're in a high-pressure situation during competition, when you're facing a particularly stressful shot, you always seem to pull it off. Those are the situations most golfers have the hardest times with. So I want to ask you a question: What do you do that makes you so good under pressure?"

Suzann stared at the ground. She looked confused. "I don't know," she said. "I've never really thought about it." Then she changed the subject. "Anyway, I'm here to work on what's wrong with my swing. It's really bothering me."

The next morning, Suzann told us she hadn't been able to sleep a wink. She said she was disturbed that she couldn't answer Pia's question. Lynn said gently, "You're telling us that you want to be an even better player than you are, but you haven't thought about what makes you so good at this game aside from your swing. We want you to keep thinking about that."

On the final morning Suzann announced, "I've been thinking about it. Here's what I know. In those pressure situations, I don't think. I just see the shot. I feel it. I don't worry about what will happen. I just go."

Suzann didn't think she had said anything profound, but we knew otherwise. In those four sentences, she had begun to deconstruct the essence of her peak performances. And she had started to use one of the critical human skills that would help her access the unique core of her talent. For the first time, she was exercising *awareness.*

In Suzann's defense, she's hardly the first golfer to lack awareness. The reality today is that many golf coaches—and even measuring devices like TrackMan—have more awareness about a player's strengths and weaknesses than the player does. Suzann was able to perform many specific golf skills, but she wasn't aware of the components of her best play on the course. We told Suzann: "Look, we get it. Golf is a solitary game. It's just you with yourself. That's why you need to heighten your awareness—internal and external—so that you can see what's *really* happening, how you really operate. Awareness creates clarity. Clarity creates choices. And choices make it possible for you to achieve the results you want."

Awareness is at the core of our teaching—and of this book. We're all different; some people are more outwardly focused, and so they're more aware of things going on around them: other competitors, the leaderboard, the wind, the golf ball, the grain or slope of the greens, the location of the target, who might be watching. They're thinking about where they want to hit their tee shot or land their ball on the green. External awareness is necessary, of course. But at the same time, outwardly focused individuals might have very little internal awareness—they might not notice that their physical energy is flagging late in the round, which emotions tend to take over on the course in certain situations (and how they affect their shots), or whether they truly have the ability to hit a hero shot.

Other people are the total opposite. They're more internally aware, which means they're very attuned to what's going on inside themselves. In terms of golf, these are intuitive players who can feel their rhythm and tempo, balance and tension, and the distance of a pitch or a putt. They're mindful of their thoughts and emotions during a round. Conversely, they might be completely unaware of their external environment. We've seen players who literally bump into other players on the tee, don't know where they're aiming, hit out of turn on a hole, walk across a fellow player's line, can't feel the wind, and completely forget their strategy for playing a hole.

We've observed that most golfers tend to have an over-developed outer awareness and an underdeveloped inner awareness. It makes sense. Considering our busy lives and the fast-paced world we live in, most of us are typically externally focused. We haven't learned how to listen to, or tune into, ourselves. In this book, we'll teach you how to build your inner awareness about your body, your mind, and your emotions. We promise that when you increase these levels of awareness, you'll see more improvement in your golf game than you would from hundreds of hours on the practice range.

But first, we need to understand what awareness is and isn't. Most golfers, in our experience, think about awareness as a swing checklist: Is my shoulder turned so that it's under my chin? Is my arm straight? Am I releasing my wrists at the right moment?

When we first take our students onto the course during our golf schools, we often ask them a series of questions to check their awareness baseline:

"Are you aware of how committed you stayed to your decision about your shot?" (Many players have never really considered the idea of commitment to their shots.)

"What percentage of your normal swing tempo did you use on that shot? 100 percent? 75 percent?" (Most golfers have little or no awareness of their normal swing tempo.)

"How are you feeling today—your body, your mind, your emotions?" (Often this question is met by nervous silence.)

"Depending on how you feel, what decisions or changes can you make that will help you play better today?" (Blank stares.)

Our good friend Dr. Debbie Crews is a sports psychology consultant for the Arizona State University men's and women's golf teams and a research analyst in kinesiology at ASU, in addition to being an LPGA Master Instructor. Debbie explains that all golfers have specific tendencies: recurring patterns that show up when they play well, and when they don't play well. Human tendencies tend to be consistent, so we can use awareness to begin to identify our tendencies—as well as the situations that trigger them. Once we do that, we can use specific human skills to manage our tendencies. In doing so, we can begin to optimize our performance.

To be fair, golf instructors and coaches have long recognized a player's tendencies in swing technique. For example, "The ball *tends* to get too far forward in your stance." Or: "You *tend* to lose your posture in the swing." "You have a *tendency* to come out of the shot before you finish your swing." But most teachers still see these tendencies as technical issues, not manifestations of a player's physical, mental, or emotional states—especially under pressure. What they don't see is that a player's grip pressure *tends* to get tight when he's looking at a par 3 over water. They don't see that a player *tends* to come out of her swing when she has been chatting with her partners and loses focus. They don't see a golfer's *tendency* for his swing tempo to increase when he is playing well, and thus starts to anticipate a low score. *In our opinion, the contexts for our tendencies are as important as the tendencies themselves.* Every golfer needs to develop an awareness of what his or her tendencies are on the golf course, and when and why they happen. This awareness can't be developed on a practice range.

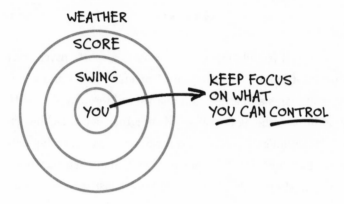

There are three areas of awareness that are critical to performing well on the golf course: physical awareness, mental awareness, and emotional awareness. Because they're interconnected, let's look at all three.

PHYSICAL AWARENESS

AT THE MOST BASIC LEVEL, physical awareness relates to the state or condition of your body at a given moment. In general, do you know if your body is flexible or inflexible? Is your center of balance high in your body, or is it low? During your warm-up before a round, do you feel energetic or lethargic? Are any of your muscles sore? Do you have an injury that hinders you? Do you feel tense or relaxed as you begin to hit balls? These physical states can affect how you play, and we want to teach you how to widen and deepen your awareness, so that you can address them properly.

MENTAL AWARENESS

THE SECOND AREA OF AWARENESS that's critical for playing good golf is mental awareness. Most of us think of mental awareness as our cognitive thoughts. There are important mental functions required to play golf that involve analyzing conditions and making decisions about shot selection and course strategy. These functions happen in the language center of our brain, which some people call the "left" or "conscious" part of the brain. The way golf has traditionally been taught tends to be a cognitive (or what we call a "neck-up") experience. We learn intellectually and factually how the club works from takeaway to finish, and in turn, we give our body specific directions to swing the club effectively.

One of the things that neuroscience research has revealed during the last several decades is that our "mental states" are comprised of far more than just the cognitive part of our brains. The "right" or "subconscious" part of the brain controls creativity, imagination, sensory abilities (seeing, hearing, feeling, touching, tasting), rhythm, music, intuition, and motor skills. Here's an important fact: The left side, or cognitive center of the brain, comprises a minuscule 5 to 10 percent of our brain power, while the right side, or creative side of the brain, comprises 90 to 95 percent of our brain power—much of which we never access. In short, we have much more potential than we are using.

Importantly, neuroscience tells us that once we've learned specific skills, if we can let go of conscious control and allow the intuitive part of our brain to take over, we can improve our performance. The highest level of execution, whether by a pianist, golfer, dancer, or skier, is controlled by the right or sensory part of the brain, and is characterized by a shift away from the conscious brain to the subconscious brain. This state is sometimes called "the zone" or "flow," and is characterized by what Dr. Crews calls "synchronicity" between the two sides

of the brain. This is the state that can, for example, most efficiently produce a golf swing that has been learned and practiced. The best athletes in the world are intuitively able to shift
from left brain to right brain at just the right time, instinctively
achieving the balance needed for peak performance. As you
become increasingly aware of different "feel" or sensory states,
we will show you how heightening some and lowering others
can help you shift into your right sensory brain and dramatically improve your performance.

EMOTIONAL AWARENESS

AN EFFECTIVE EXERCISE we like to use with our students is
asking them to recall any emotions they associate with beginning to learn the game—especially if they were children at
the time. Often these feelings are intrinsic joyful states, and
they're extremely powerful. Whether it was the special time
you spent with your father or mother on the course, or shag-
ging balls on the range in the afternoon for pocket change,
these emotions are often at the root of why we play.

Amy Lane, a 5-handicap from New York who plays golf on
Long Island, says she can vividly recall how she felt as a young
golfer. "I remember coming home from camp when I was
about 13 years old. My parents signed me up for a junior clinic
at the golf club in New Jersey where they were members," she
says. "An assistant pro took an interest in me. We'd go out onto
the course late in the afternoon, and I'd carry my bag on my
back. I don't really remember the specifics of the lessons, but
I remember how free I felt on those days. I would feel happy,
and I would play well. They were always connected for me. I

never focused on my bad shots. I was always excited about my good shots and how much fun I was having."

Another of our students, PGA Tour pro Russell Knox, remembers learning to play in his native Scotland. "I grew up in a town called Nairn Dunbar in the Scottish Highlands," he says. "The course didn't even have a driving range close by. My friends and I would just go out and chop it around and try to put the ball in the hole. The weather was often terrible—cold, rainy, and windy. We'd get beaten up by the elements, but I always had this feeling of joy out there. We *played*, in the best sense of the word. Today, even with all the stress and expectations that go with being a professional golfer, I still try to access that feeling of joy I had in my body when I was a kid."

As Amy grew older, she sought more lessons to improve, which led to a more technical focus on her game—and less joy. "My teachers would instruct me, 'You're in this position or that position. Try this instead.' I developed a tendency to overthink my swing and my shots," she says. "If I was playing poorly, I'd start to get anxious and cycle through my Rolodex of swing thoughts. *Do this. But it's not working. Do that. Now what?* It was the exact opposite of how I felt as a kid. And it just about killed my game."

Amy came to her first VISION54 program in 2006. "I started becoming more aware of how my emotions affected my play," she says. "I would start a downward spiral during a round. I'd get tight. Then I'd try to force some technical swing fix. Of course, it never worked. Once I became aware of how anxiety and tension were affecting me, I began to be able to address it. I stopped freaking out about my swing technique. Instead, I tried to access the sensory *feeling* I have in my body when I hit a great shot. For me, it's an awareness of a low center of gravity below my belly button. I feel balanced. Everything gets simple, and time slows down. I can actually see and feel my shot before I hit the ball. I'm in the present, not distracted by thoughts about my swing. I regain my confidence. Awareness helps me reset my equilibrium."

We believe that the role of emotions is underappreciated in golf. When someone hits a wayward shot, we almost always see an emotional reaction: head shaking, groaning, club dropping, bag-kicking, sighing, cursing, etc. Emotions can manifest as anxiety ("Oh no, I'm in the bunker"), or defeat ("I'm hitting the ball so badly I'm going in"), or futility ("Why even bother playing this game?"). For some players, a flood of emotions can quickly overwhelm their game, and send them into acute distress.

When we hit good shots, we tend to react with positive emotions. We smile, we high-five, we fist-pump. All emotions trigger a chemical reaction in the brain that directly affects how we perform. Events that we "emotionalize" (positively or negatively) are stored in the amygdala, the area deep in our brains that processes memory and emotional reactions. When we have similar shots in the future, we will feel confidence, trust, and a "go" signal or, conversely, anxiety and lack of confidence.

In everyday life, we recognize somebody's intense emotions as authenticity. But there are situations in which it is extremely valuable to be able to manage your emotions. Managing emotions can reduce irritation and anger, and create peace of mind, which facilitates a generalized happy state—and better performance.

"When you're competing in a stressful match or about to hit an important shot, it's sometimes easier to try to control your technique than your emotions," observes Amy. "We work on so many aspects of our swings in golf. But we rarely work on controlling our emotions."

It is essential that a golfer be in good physical, mental, and emotional states to play well. Your physical state is where you want to start developing awareness, because it will be what sets the tone for your round as you hit your first several balls. This is why we begin our VISION54 programs with what we call "BTT Awareness Drills" (you'll read more about them in Chapter 3). BTT stands for Balance, Tempo, and Tension, and by paying attention to these sensory states in your warm-up and during your round, you will be accessing your sensory awareness, which will help you access the right side of your brain and promote better swings.

At the start of our programs, we ask students to try out different sensory states on the range and on the course. Some of these are kinesthetic feels (balance, relaxed shoulders, and grip pressure). Others are auditory (singing a song, counting your swing tempo, or listening to the sound of impact). Still others are visual (looking at the ball or seeing the ball flight or the target). States can be emotional, too (feeling joy or calm). Beginning to explore these states is the start to developing inner awareness.

Suzann Pettersen asked us to work individually with her in early 2007, shortly after she had attended our VISION54 program. The first assignment we gave her was to become more aware of what she did when she played her best—the original question she'd been unable to answer. She knew her strengths were her swing technique and fitness, but she was able to realize she was often overly focused on technical swing issues, which meant she spent too much time concentrating in the language center of her brain. Suzann needed to access more of her right-brain sensory states when she played. One thing we asked her to do was to putt with her eyes closed. When she did, she was able to let go of technical thoughts and access a "feel" state of putting—*sensing* the distance, *sensing* the break, *sensing* the speed of the putt, and trusting her gut instincts.

Another area we worked on with Suzann was emotional awareness. Suzann was very emotionally volatile when she competed. After a good shot, she'd be confident and exuberant, but if she hit a bad shot, her shoulders would slump and she might slam her club on the ground. There were times, we joked, that she looked like a Viking warrior with fire coming out of her nostrils. When she reacted this way, it didn't matter that her technique and her fitness were superior. Her emotions interfered so much with her brain and her body that they effectively took down her entire game.

Suzann needed to develop awareness of her emotional tendencies during competition and learn to manage them. She needed to disrupt her negative reactions as soon as they started. We suggested she count to herself after every shot— good or bad. *One one-thousand, two one-thousand, three one-thousand, four one-thousand, five one-thousand.* Counting is an age-old anger-management technique, and it works for a reason. When a person gets angry, the amygdala fires hot, sending out stress hormones such as adrenaline and cortisol that prepare the body for its "fight or flight" responses. The heart rate increases, breathing becomes rapid, and glucose levels rise. If we don't interrupt this response when it occurs, it will interfere with our ability to think, and to hit the ball.

Suzann is a quick study. When we told her about the amygdala firing after a bad shot and the need to offset her negative reaction by "storing" a positive memory, she said wryly, "I've never stored anything positive in my whole life. How long is this going to take?"

It didn't take long. Suzann gained awareness of her tendencies toward anger and frustration in competition and learned how to manage them. Within a few months, she was seeing a dramatic improvement in her performance. In June 2007, she won the Michelob ULTRA Open at Kingsmill, Virginia, her first LPGA Tour victory. One month later, she won her first major, the LPGA Championship, by one stroke over Karrie Webb. This moved her to No. 4 in the world rankings. That summer, Suzann also won the SAS Open on the Ladies European Tour, which she followed with her third, fourth, and fifth LPGA Tour victories. In December, she reached her career-high ranking of No. 2 in the world.

At the end of that year someone asked us, "How did Suzann improve so much and so quickly?" We answered, "One of the things she did was to develop a new performance skill to advance her game. It's called awareness."

FOUNDATIONAL HUMAN SKILLS: AWARENESS

ONE OF THE GOLFERS we had the privilege of coaching was former PGA Tour player Arron Oberholser, who is now a commentator for Golf Channel. Arron picked up the importance of awareness on the course right away, so we'll let him describe it.

"Awareness means you're noticing the things around you— which means you're in the present moment," he explains. "Whenever I wasn't playing well, I knew it was because I was thinking ahead to my final score, or thinking back to a mediocre shot. When this happened, I used a trick which I still use today. I would say, *'Arron, where are you?'* I'd say it aloud, although softly enough that my competitors couldn't hear me. It could have been during the first round on a Thursday morning or during the final round on a Sunday afternoon. Then I would go into a deep description to myself about where I was on the course and what was happening. *I'm here on the 5th hole, I've got a slightly downhill lie, I've got 27 yards to the hole. The wind is coming from the left, the greens are firm, and the pin is on the right. I feel focused. It's a beautiful, sunny day.* Doing this always brought me back to the present."

Arron adds, "The present is all there is in golf. There's nothing else. The more you can figure out how to get yourself to the present during your round, the better you'll play. The fun part for each player is to find his or her own path to the present."

AWARENESS

TRAINING THE ABILITY to access your awareness is something you need to practice regularly. Repeated practice will strengthen your inner- and outer-awareness skills. You'll begin to recognize your physical, mental, and emotional states, and your tendencies in each of them on the golf course. At first, you'll experience brief moments of what is called "integration"—when all your states are in harmony. These brief moments will become longer. Eventually, you'll learn to access each particular awareness state at will and be able to manage each of them.

The challenge is how well you can stay present throughout your entire shot. Begin with these awareness questions and on-course explorations. Even if you can't answer them all right away, think of them as little seedlings that will open and grow as you practice. Write down your observations in a notebook.

GENERAL QUESTIONS

- Are you a more outwardly aware or inwardly aware person?
- Is your mind typically focused or scattered?
- Do you tend to be positive or negative about yourself?
- Are your emotions on the course generally calm, excited, nervous, worried, or confident?
- What are you internally aware of during your swing? Is it technical? A feeling in your body? The target?
- Are you aware of how your body feels from day to day? Do you keep track of tightness, energy levels, tension, and balance?
- Do you make a plan for how to play the course each time you go out?
- What is your self-talk? (That is, What do you say to yourself before or after a shot?)
- What do you feel emotionally before, during, or after a shot?
- How do you prepare for each shot?
- How do you typically react to your shots?

OUTER AWARENESS

- How often do you pay attention to something on the course, such as a tree, mounds, a bunker, the grain of the grass, or the wind?
- What external conditions are you aware of before deciding on your shot?
- Do you notice where other players in your group hit their shots?
- How clear is your target on each shot?
- Is it easy or difficult for you to remember your score?

INNER AWARENESS

- What do you feel internally during your swing?
- Can you tell before a shot if you have trusted the decision you've made?
- Can you tell after the shot if you trusted your decision?
- Can you identify your emotional reaction after a shot?
- Describe the state of your body at various points during your round: Was it relaxed, tense, tired, or energized? Were you hungry, satiated, or thirsty?
- Describe the state of your mind at various points during your round: Were you distracted, confused, focused, or clear?
- Describe your emotions at various points during your round: Were you confident, happy, annoyed, frustrated, angry, or calm?

INNER AND OUTER AWARENESS: ON-COURSE EXPLORATIONS

PLAY NINE HOLES, and explore one of these ideas on each hole. Write down your answers in a notebook.

1. Play a hole where you are extroverted, and talk between shots.

2. Play a hole where you are introverted, and don't talk between shots.

Which style do you prefer?

3. Play a hole hitting each shot toward a small and detailed target.

4. Play a hole hitting each shot toward a more general target area.

Which do you prefer?

5. Play a hole making a practice swing before each swing or stroke.

6. Play a hole with no practice swings.

Which works better for you?

7. Play a hole using strong body language and a confident voice between shots.

8. Play a hole pretending to be weak and unclear about your choices and swings between shots.

What differences did you notice?

9. Play a hole and alternate hitting a shot with 100-percent commitment and a shot with weak or indecisive commitment.

What differences do you notice as you alternate shots?

PIA: THE ACCIDENTAL COACH

WAS A SHY INTROVERT when I left Sweden at age 19 to attend Arizona State University and play on the golf team. I liked to read and study, and I was good at math and physics, so I started as a pre-medicine student with the intention of becoming a doctor, like my father. But the pre-med classes conflicted with golf practice, so I began taking other courses that interested me—philosophy, psychology, anatomy . . . those sorts of subjects. I was curious. I wanted to be able to figure out things for myself.

After college, I qualified for the LPGA Tour. In terms of awareness, I had always been taught by my instructors to have specific "swing thoughts" and to "think" those thoughts when I played. I practiced hard and used all my willpower to stay within my thoughts, especially during competition. Though I was making cuts in these events, I didn't play to the level I wanted. Like Suzann Pettersen, I was disappointed in myself and confused about why I wasn't performing better. I was practicing hard, my swing was good, and I was physically fit. So why wasn't I winning? It was driving me crazy.

After more than four years on tour, I took a break in March 1987 and went back to Sweden for a couple of months of soul-searching. When I got home, I was totally unprepared for the reception I received. Because I was among the first generation of Swedish golfers to play American college golf and then professionally, I was a celebrity. The Swedish PGA and the Swedish Golf Federation showered me with invitations: Could you do clinics for our junior golfers? Would you speak at our awards dinner? Would you join our tournament and rules committees?

I gave talks, met with officials, and started helping with our national teams. It was fun, and suddenly my experiences started making sense. To stay sharp, I entered a few Swedish tournaments—and guess what? I started winning. I began to play the way I had wanted to play in the States, relatively pressure free. Amazingly, I did it while practicing less, working out less, and most importantly, *thinking* less about my game. Maybe I was playing better because I had other interests, new challenges and voyages of discovery that made me eager to get up in the morning. One day, the head coach of the Swedish women's national team quit. I agreed to become the interim coach, telling myself I'd do it for a little while until I went back to the LPGA Tour.

I started working with Sweden's elite women golfers, among them a shy 18-year-old named Annika Sorenstam. Two questions occurred to me immediately. The first was, *Can we change the way we coach so that the next generation of Swedish players succeeds professionally at the international level?* The second question was, *What can we do to help these elite golfers become better and happier human beings?*

One of the first things I did was establish a routine of following my players around the golf course. I went out with a notebook and simply jotted down what I observed—the tempo of their swings, whether they were talkative or quiet, the quality of their shots, and especially, how they reacted to their shots. (Most of the golfers I observed lacked emotional awareness and self-management skills, and became frustrated and angry when they hit a bad shot.) I timed each player's pre-shot routine, initially from a pace-of-play perspective, but also suspecting that elaborate preparation was counterproductive. This kind of observation was becoming routine in business, where efficiency experts ran time-and-motion studies to increase the effectiveness of production. No one had yet thought to apply it to golf.

I wasn't sophisticated, but I was smart enough to know from experience that hitting golf balls on a practice range and playing on the course were two very different things. With my notes in hand, I was able to give a player some feedback that was more than just technical at the end of her round: "You were chatting like a magpie when you made those birdies," or: "You stood still over the ball for 14 seconds before you drove it into the lake." I'd say, "Let's think about how you can use this information." Then I shared it with the players' club pros at home. I did all this simply because it made sense to me. I figured golfers needed different kinds of knowledge and skills to help them during competition. Certainly, I had needed it. Now I couldn't stop thinking about what the next generation of Swedish golfers could achieve with an entirely different kind of coaching.

During this period, I ran into Patty Sheehan, one of the LPGA's biggest stars, at a tournament. "What are you doing, Pia? When are you coming back?" she asked.

"I don't know," I said. "Soon, I guess."

But I never went back. Because now I was a coach. I had a group of Sweden's top golfers with whom I could experiment. My Swedish friend Charlotte Montgomery, who played golf with me at ASU and on the LPGA Tour, became my assistant. We read voraciously in the fields of golf instruction, coaching, psychology, management, and self-help. Stephen Covey's book *The Seven Habits of Highly Effective People* had a lot to say about self-discovery, self-mastery, prioritizing, and physical and mental renewal. I read Chuck Hogan's booklet *Practice Golf.* He was one of the first "outside the box" golf instructors, so I was interested in his perspective. I also read performance coach Tony Robbins's book *Unlimited Power.*

I was fortunate. After a few years, the Swedish Golf Federation appointed me head coach for all men's and women's national teams, including professional players. And they left me alone. I had no bosses telling me what I could or couldn't do. The players started shooting lower scores and winning tournaments. So the Swedish Golf directors sort of shrugged and said, "We don't know what you're doing, but it seems to be working. Keep on doing it."

I continued to be curious. I kept being open to new ideas, and I committed to the belief that players will become more aware, and take responsibility for making their own decisions, if we coaches encourage them. Our group of coaches had a simple vision: Players can achieve their potential as human beings through the experience of playing golf.

CHAPTER 2

VARIABILITY:
WELCOME TO THE GAME OF GOLF

O NE OF THE COOLEST THINGS about the first tee is that it's a metaphor for what lies ahead of us—on the course and within ourselves. Whether we're professionals, low-handicap amateurs, or weekend players, we've got 18 opportunities to get the ball in the hole. Along the way, we'll encounter good and bad lies, difficult and easy pin positions, fast and slow greens, and pleasant or unpleasant weather and playing partners. Did we mention that we have no control over any of this? How we approach (and manage) lucky and unlucky bounces—internal and external—is part of the seductive (or maddening) mystery of the game.

As the Greek philosopher Heraclitus famously said, "A person cannot step into the same river twice." If we walk down to the bank of a river, the water that flows by isn't the same water that flowed by a minute before. Let's say we step into the river, then step out. When we step in a second time, are we literally stepping into a different river? As human beings, with our states, moods, even the cells in our bodies changing from minute to minute, are we also different people as we step in and out of the river? Ever-present change is a constant in our world. That, too, is how it is to be a river. And, we might add, a golfer.

At VISION54, we've given this state of perpetual change our own word: *variability*.

Why is the idea of variability so critical for golfers to understand? In our opinion, too many players focus on achieving
"consistency." They practice the same shots and swings over and
over, convinced that more time on the range will enable them
to perfectly replicate a swing that will never let them down. But
scientific research now shows that endless hours on the range
are ineffective. In 2006, Stanford University's Krishna Shenoy,
a professor of electrical engineering and neurobiology, showed
that humans aren't capable of perfectly replicating a physical
action. Shenoy, who studies the neural basis of movement, explained: "The main reason you can't move the same way each
and every time—when you're swinging a golf club, say—is that
your brain can't plan the swing the same way each time."

Professor Shenoy and two colleagues, Mark Churchland and
Afsheen Afshar, published the study in the scientific journal
Neuron. The team trained rhesus macaque monkeys to repeat
the simple task of reaching toward a colored spot on a screen
and touching it thousands of times. They rewarded the monkeys for completing the task at varying speeds. But the monkeys were never able to consistently repeat the same movement
with the same speed. The problem couldn't be corrected with
more practice. The scientists concluded that the brain has
evolved this improvisational and inexact movement pattern
because a majority of situations require us to produce unique
motions. Our survival depends on it. Predators never get the
chance to catch and kill prey in exactly the same way under
the exact same conditions; likewise, prey doesn't survive by
evading predators in exactly the same manner. "The nervous
system was designed to be flexible, not to do the same thing
over and over," Churchland explained when the study was pub-

lished. Given this, the scientists extrapolated, an athlete's quest for consistency is at odds with how human brains have evolved. "The pervasive belief that we can repeat our [golf] swings is wrong; science tells us the brain will *never* allow this to happen. If we accept that our swings will always be variable day to day, then the way we practice can become more productive. Golf is a random game played in an ever-changing and flexible environment. Yet players spend hours on the practice range hitting ball after ball in a fixed and closed environment. Players should spend more time simulating the real game."

A scientist said that. Hallelujah!

HAVE YOU EVER TOSSED a few blades of grass into the air to see how the wind has changed in the seconds since your partner hit his or her shot? Have you hit a perfect shot, only to see your ball strike a sprinkler head and bounce into the water hazard? Have you been confused after playing beautifully one day, then barely hitting the ball the next? Your scorecard might read 84 on two consecutive days, but the journeys to getting there look entirely different.

Variability is the one constant in golf. First we want you to acknowledge this. Then we want you to truly embrace it. And finally, we want you to become what we call a Master of Variability.

On the first day of our VISION54 schools, we draw a diagram on our whiteboard for our students. On one side is a big circle we label PRACTICE. Inside the circle we write the four things we need to play good golf: Technique (a reliable swing), Fitness (your body's physical ability), Equipment (clubs that fit you), and Human Skills (the ability to manage yourself physically, mentally, and emotionally).

The first question we ask is this: Once you step onto the first tee, which of these four things can you truly influence while playing? Your technical skills? If you can't hit a flop shot or a draw, it won't magically appear, so we erase technique. Are you golf-fit? If you haven't trained properly, stamina and flexibility aren't going to suddenly materialize. That gets erased, too. How about your equipment? Unfortunately, you can't call for a new set of clubs on the course, so we erase equipment.

Only one of our original four is left: Your *human skills* are what you can truly manage on the course.

So instead of fighting variability, embrace it. By letting go of what you can't control and focusing on what you can, you will come closer to achieving what golfers call "consistency."

Annika Sorenstam was the greatest Master of Variability we've ever seen. "If something changed during a round,

I always knew I had to adjust right away," she explains. "It could've been the weather, or the course conditions, or my mood. I might have been playing with a slow player one round, then with a fast player the next round. Or, I was playing in a tournament, and play was suspended by a storm. I used to watch other players get upset and say, 'I was playing so well! Now I'm going to lose it.' They allowed external change to disrupt them. No matter what happened, I always tried to stick to my routine. You need something you can count on. That's your foundation. Change never freaked me out. I always tried to stay focused on the present, on what I could control—which was myself." In other words, Annika used her human skills to manage variability. And she won 90 tournaments during her career, the most of any professional woman golfer in history.

One of the most impressive examples of mastering variability occurred in 2003 when Annika was invited to play in the PGA Tour's Bank of America Colonial in Fort Worth, Texas. The tournament organizers had a tradition of inviting exceptional golfers who otherwise wouldn't have qualified to play. Annika was 32 years old at the time and the No. 1–ranked woman in the world. She was a veteran competitor, the winner of 43 titles, four major championships, and five-time Player of the Year honors on the LPGA Tour. Annika was always interested in creating new goals and pushing her boundaries. She would be competing against the best male golfers in the game, and would be the first woman to play in a men's tour event since Babe Didrikson Zaharias in 1945.

The day Annika accepted the invitation, she called Pia on the telephone. "What do you think is going to happen there?" she asked.

"Well, no one knows," Pia answered. "But it's still going to be the same you with your same tendencies. The pressure will probably amplify those tendencies, but you don't have to suddenly worry that you're going to turn into a different person. It's still you. Just practice with that in mind."

That's what Annika did. Being an analytical person, she researched everything and tried to anticipate what she might encounter that would be different. "There was a lot of ruckus on the PGA Tour when they announced I was going to play," she recalls. "Vijay Singh withdrew from the tournament, and Nick Price said I was looking for publicity. There were oddsmakers in Las Vegas taking bets about whether I would make the cut or miss the first fairway. It got so crazy that I stopped reading the Internet and newspapers. I didn't want to let that distract me."

Annika talked with people about what the atmosphere and the crowds would be like. She called Billie Jean King, the tennis champion who had played her own "Battle of the Sexes" match against Bobby Riggs 30 years earlier. "I tried to visualize myself in a media circus that was bigger than the U.S. Open, bigger than anything I had experienced," she says.

She researched PGA Tour players' routines on the first tee to see how they were different from the women's tour. "I know it sounds silly, but I got a PGA Tour pin sheet to see what it looked like. I tried to reduce the variabilities that would surprise me."

Annika would be playing a course that was 500 to 800 yards longer than she was used to playing. "I put in the time in the gym. I played from the back tees on my home course. I really prepared. When I got there, I felt ready."

On the first day of the tournament Pia was standing near the putting green at Colonial Country Club. "Annika came up to me before going to the tee," Pia says. "She was so nervous, she could hardly talk. I told her, 'No matter what happens today, Nelson will still love you.' Nelson was her cat. She let out a big sigh of relief and said, 'You're right, Pia.' Then she walked to the tee."

"How many first tee shots had I hit in my life? Probably thousands," Annika says. "In some ways, hitting your first shot of the day is always the same, but always different. The first tee experience at Colonial was the most extreme I've ever faced. The environment was different, the PGA Tour crowd was different, the yardages were different. I felt I could deal with those things; it was the stakes and the expectations that were so new to me."

Annika prepared to tee off on the 10th hole. She looked down the fairway and saw photographers and spectators hanging from the trees. "I was like *Wow, okay,*" she says. "Once they called my name, I just stuck to my routine. I was actually more nervous about teeing up the ball than hitting the shot. You know when your hands are shaking? I knew I couldn't have Terry [McNamara], my caddie, tee up the ball for me. How would that look? So once I got the ball on the tee, the worst was over. That was the most stressful part."

Preparing to hit, she told herself it was an ordinary shot. "As crazy as it sounds, it helped me stay focused. I told myself all the usual things: *You've hit your 4-wood thousands of times; the ball doesn't know it's at Colonial; focus on your shot and not on your surroundings.*"

Annika had a pre-shot routine of 24 seconds. She generally spent 20 seconds making her decision about the shot and four seconds over the ball before she hit. Terry told her afterward that her routine had been 23½ seconds, which considering the circumstances was extraordinary. With a 4-wood, she ripped her tee shot about 255 yards, 30 yards farther than normal. "I stayed with the things that were under my control," she says. "Once the ball hit the fairway, I could enjoy the day—a little bit."

Annika's goal was to shoot par on the 7,080-yard course. She finished the round with a one-over-par 71, an impressive feat under such enormous pressure. She missed only one fairway and putted for birdie on every hole, making one birdie and two bogeys. And though she missed the cut the next day, shooting a 74, she accomplished what she had set out to do: manage herself in a new, challenging situation and hold her own against the best men golfers in the world.

One reason Annika mastered variability more quickly than her opponents was her honesty. She'd say, "I feel super nervous," acknowledging the feeling right away before her nervous system got overloaded. People sometimes observed that Annika was machine-like. It wasn't that she lacked emotions. She had a simple structure that allowed her to say, *Okay, Annika, what's happening? What are you feeling? What is under your control? And what can you do about it?* If she was nervous, she would count the dimples on her golf ball while waiting to tee off or between holes. Or she'd think about cooking or decorating her house. Or she'd internally recite a mantra: *Fairways and greens, fairways and greens.* Everyone said Annika was so consistent. We knew that wasn't true. She was simply better at managing external and internal variabilities during a round. That helped her avoid mistakes and blow-up holes, and produced more consistent outcomes.

It really doesn't matter whether you're Annika Sorenstam, a beginner, or an intermediate golfer. Knowing your tendencies and what is and isn't under your control will help put you on the path to mastering variability—the ultimate metaphor for golf.

FOUNDATIONAL HUMAN SKILLS: MASTERING VARIABILITY

GOLFERS TEND TO PRACTICE the same things over and over on the range. But players need to explore variability on the course, where the game happens. When golfers come to our VISION54 school, they go out on the course on the first day to play several holes. We want to observe their skills in the context of the game.

It's important to practice the reality of variability. Many golfers give themselves a perfect lie on the practice range and hit ball after ball. Then they get on the course and say, "Oh no! My ball is in a divot" or "A tree is blocking my path to the hole." They don't have the skills to manage variability, so they complain and blame their technique.

Practice uphill and downhill lies; play from different tee boxes, mix up the clubs you hit off the tee (say, a driver and fairway wood). Play three, six, or nine holes with the intention of getting the ball to the back of the green on every approach shot. (Most players tend to go short on greens, so this exercise makes you aware of how much space you have behind the flag and how much more club you would need to get to the back of the green.)

As with awareness, variability can be external or internal. External variability is wind and cold weather; it's grass that has dew on it or that has been mowed recently. It's the grain of the greens. External variability can include the pace of play of your group, or your spouse giving you unwanted advice during the round, or your parents standing in the gallery with their arms sternly folded across their chests.

Internal variability includes the ever-changing state of your body, your mind, and your emotions. If you are aware of these changes, you'll understand how and why your swing can feel so different each day.

Exploring internal variability might require a bit of acting. If you don't like slow play, then add extra time before each shot and notice where your anxiety starts to build. Experiment with focusing on something to distract you from your frustration. If you don't like playing at a fast pace, go out and play six holes of speed golf. Rush yourself between shots, and learn to manage your reactions. As you can see, variability is infinite. Look at it as fun, and practice it!

MASTERING VARIABILITY: QUESTIONS

- How do you react to slow play?
- How do you react to fast play?
- How do you react when you get unlucky bounces or bad lies?
- How do you feel when you start off your round well—or badly?
- How do you perform with different kinds of players and personalities?
- How do you perform on different types of courses?
- How do you react when your swing feels different from day to day?

• How well do you manage changes in your body, mind, and emotions during a round?

MASTERING VARIABILITY: ON-COURSE EXPLORATIONS

PLAY NINE HOLES, and practice one of these explorations on each hole.

1. On one hole, hit a shot you wouldn't normally hit with a particular club. Stay committed.

2. On one hole, pick something that distracts you (such as other players talking or moving behind you, branches or twigs in your line of sight, etc.). How effective are you at remaining focused?

3. On one hole, play speed golf. Run, jog, or walk fast between shots, and stick to the shortest routine possible. How do you perform when you have to speed up?

4. Make one hole a slow-play hole where you add two or three minutes before each shot; feel where your anxiety or irritation starts to build. Notice it. Practice how to deal with it. How good are you at remaining focused when it's your turn to hit?

5. Play one hole from a different tee box. Notice how the holes set up differently, and how you change your approach.

6. If you normally tee off with a driver on one hole, tee off with a 4-wood instead. Play the hole with a different strategy than you'd normally use. How does it change the way you play?

7. Play a hole and give yourself bad lies on all shots. See how you can regroup and hit a decent shot.

8. Play a hole feeling tight in your body. What shots can you hit in this state that are good enough?

9. Play a hole doing some high-leg lifts or jumping jacks before your pre-shot routine to increase your adrenaline. Notice what puts you into a good state before you hit.

What did you learn about yourself and your game by doing these exercises?

LYNN: THE MAD GENIUS
OF CHUCK HOGAN

I N THE SPRING OF 1995, Chuck Hogan gave a seminar at a hotel in Tempe, Arizona, one of many that I helped facilitate. Chuck, one of the most original golf teachers of our generation, had been shaken by a debilitating attack of nerves when he was a junior golfer. He'd made it his life's work to explore what he half-jokingly called "the devil that possessed the body and mind of every athlete who failed to live up to their known performance baseline."

Technical mastery offered false hope, Chuck said, because hard work and repetition were never a match for the free-floating anxiety that plagued golfers.

"Why," Chuck would ask, "does a 55-year-old CEO of a billion-dollar company become a quivering bundle of nerves on the golf course? Is it fear of failure? Fear of success? No," he'd explain. "It's the haunting concern: What if I miss? What will they think of me?" Performance, in Chuck's view, would always be hostage to our self-consciousness. "If we can't be secure enough to swing at a golf ball," he wondered, "then where and when can we be secure?"

I first met Chuck at a PGA of America seminar in Palm Beach Gardens, Florida, in 1987. He was 37 years old at the time, and he was already a maverick in our profession. Chuck was there to talk about how golf instructors needed to look at a person's behavior if they wanted to be effective teachers. If we were going to help players improve and enjoy the game more, he said, we needed to look at them as human beings with individual strengths, weaknesses, and vulnerabilities—not just assess the technical details of their golf swings.

I thought, "Of course!" But golf pros didn't "do" psychology in those days, and our formal PGA of America training had taught us that when giving a golf lesson, you were there to address the swing: the grip, the swing plane, and the hinging of the wrists on the backswing. Chuck became the next step in my evolution from swing teacher to performance coach.

At that time in my career, I was teaching at a club called Frenchman's Creek in Florida during the winter and at the Kittansett Golf Club near Cape Cod in the summer. It was a perfect life. At Frenchman's, I was working alongside the famous teaching pro Jack Grout, who was Jack Nicklaus's coach. At Kittansett, the pro was a brilliant and quirky man named Tom Shea. (Members would come off the course requesting a ruling from Tom, and the assistant would say, "Oh, Tom's upstairs meditating.")

As inspiring as Jack and Tom were, eventually I wanted a different challenge. In 1988, I decided to upend my life and go to work for Chuck Hogan in Sedona, Arizona. I had no guaranteed income, but I moved anyway and became the lead instructor at his golf school, Sports Enhancement Associates (SEA).

My friends and family thought I was nuts, and I can't blame them. Chuck was seen as somewhat of a mad genius. I went with him to the PGA Teaching & Coaching Summit in 1988, where as part of our presentation, I put on a silly costume and went onstage as a character called Balata Hacknomore from the planet Flog. Chuck, who like Tom Shea was influenced by Michael Murphy, co-founder of the Esalen Institute in California, and an influential figure in the Human Potential Movement, talked about "optimal performance states." Most of his presentations probably came off as total debunking of traditional golf instruction. I admired Chuck. He was unconventional—and fun. Unfortunately, his lack of diplomacy had consequences. Chuck had so many run-ins with the PGA of America hierarchy that they finally kicked him out of the organization.

Chuck was working with quite a few PGA Tour players at the time. He was one of the first to introduce the concept of compartmentalizing the routine. Chuck knew how different brainwave states affected performance. He talked about shifting from a left-brain state to a right-brain state. Optimal performance, he said, occurred at infrequent times when athletes functioned in an almost unconscious and effortless state that was super-clear and focused. Chuck used hypnotism to get players into this state; sometimes they would then go out and win a tournament. But because the players didn't understand how they had accessed the state (and therefore couldn't replicate it on their own), it all remained mysterious to them. This wasn't very practical, because it required players to come back to Chuck, who was out there embracing his inner guru, talking in parables, speaking a language that tour pros didn't understand. Players got a glimpse of their true potential, but they didn't learn skills to realize that potential independently.

That's how my role evolved. I became a bridge between Chuck and his students. I explained his program and techniques in language that was more down-to-earth and relevant to their experience of golf. After all, those tour players weren't paying Chuck to teach them the meaning of life. They just wanted to play the 72nd hole without throwing up on themselves.

Chuck always encouraged me to dig deeper into the mysteries of performance. He, Tom Shea, and I once took a trip to the Esalen Institute in Big Sur, California, where thinkers like Michael Murphy and others were pondering the idea of human potential. We toured the grounds and soaked in Esalen's famous hot springs as waves crashed on the nearby rocks. I was thrilled to meet people who were willing to journey toward the edge—literally—of human possibility.

Was I a seeker? I guess I was. I was also a dabbler and an investigator. Forgive me for saying this, but helping people with their golf swings was boring. Fixing a swing didn't help anyone become a better person, or improve a life. I had a stubborn belief that golf could be a vehicle for self-discovery. Chuck was amazingly courageous. My experience with him shifted my paradigm of what I believed was possible for human beings—including golfers.

CHAPTER 3

PERFORMANCE STATE 101:
BALANCE, TEMPO, AND TENSION

THE PRACTICE RANGE at a professional tournament is a fascinating place to watch the best players in the world work on their games. On a Monday before the tournament, players tend to be pretty relaxed, joking with one another as they go through their routines. Tuesdays are generally calm, too. By Wednesday, you can see the players starting to get a little edgy. On Thursday, the start of the tournament, they're certifiably antsy. Our colleague David Leadbetter describes the players he coaches on "a scale of relaxation" during tournament week. During the early practice days, he tries to help them get to what he calls a state of "feel" in which they're comfortable. "Players take in information differently," he explains. "With some players I might say very little: 'That swing looks good, aim a little over to the right there. Perfect.' I might tell another player: 'Listen, you took about five seconds more than you normally do on those last few shots.' Often players aren't aware of shifts in their routines that can be very subtle; the wind might be blowing in a direction that he doesn't like, or there's a pin position on a certain hole she knows will make her uncomfortable. If you watch the pros practice, you can see whether they're trying to hone an aspect of technique or grooving a sense of rhythm or balance."

The 2015 PGA Championship at Whistling Straits in Kohler,

Wisconsin, was a particularly interesting place to watch different players' practice routines. At the range on Thursday morning, Rory McIlroy, the World No. 1 player at the time, was hitting ball after ball with his driver. Rory was returning from a five-week layoff after rupturing ligaments in his ankle while playing soccer. You could tell his practice involved testing the stability of that ankle. Next to Rory on the range was the 30-year-old Scotsman Russell Knox, whom we coach. Russell was doing something so unusual in his warm-up that spectators started gathering behind him to watch. First he hit a series of balls with his feet close together. Next he raised his left foot off the ground behind him and, while standing on his right leg, hit a series of balls one-handed with just his left arm. Afterward, he switched sides, standing on his left leg and hitting balls with only his right arm. The coordination and control he had over his body were impressive. "At first I was self-conscious because my warm-up is so different from everybody else's," Russell laughs. "Guys would walk by me and say, 'What the hell are you doing?' After a while, I just learned to answer very politely, 'Mind your own business.'"

Russell was warming up with his VISION54 "BTT skills"—exercises that activate a player's balance, tempo, and tension awareness. Being able to feel balance, tempo, and tension is key to a golfer's inner awareness—and we think this is crucial to the fundamentals of golf. First and foremost, balance, tempo, and tension are key elements of a good swing. What Russell was doing on the range was activating his athleticism and creating confidence. Understanding that his body changed from day to day, he was using the exercises to "dial in" what felt right that day.

Balance, tempo, and tension exercises will help you coordinate the proper sequence of your swing. Your grip pressure, balance, and the tempo of your backswing and forward swing must function together to deliver the club to the ball. Balance, tempo, and tension are sensory-based stimuli; that is, they are noncognitive, and focusing on them will help move you to the right or unconscious side of your brain (the side that produces the most efficient athletic movement) as you prepare to hit. Just as important, when you encounter pressure or stress on the golf course, accessing awareness of your balance, tempo, and tension levels—even stepping to the side and taking one swing with your feet together—can help reset your best physical, mental, and emotional states.

But let's back up. Russell first contacted us in 2009 for help with his game. At the time, he was playing on the mini-tours, trying to climb his way up to the Web.com Tour, which is the top developmental tour for the PGA Tour. We could see that Russell had great natural talent, but he was getting in his own way. "Everybody always talks about the swing in golf—that if you have a nice swing, you're automatically going to be good," Russell says. "Well, I had a good swing, but I was doing everything else horribly. I would get way too upset and angry if things didn't go my way on the course or if I hit poor shots. I would let one bad shot carry over to the next hole, and the next hole, and before you knew it, I had wasted three or four holes. Pia and Lynn helped me think about other aspects of the game besides the swing. I woke up to the importance of my attitude, my body language, my balance, tempo, and tension, and my pre- and post-shot reactions. I quickly understood that they were often more important than the shot itself."

TECHNICAL HUMAN
SKILLS + SKILLS
= PERFORMANCE

Russell worked on his balance, swing tempo, and tension for a few weeks. "I saw immediate results," he says. "It's so simple. When I focused on them, I wasn't overthinking my shots or getting anxious or upset." His game felt so good, he took a gamble and decided to skip the mini-tour circuit and try to compete in the higher-level Web.com Tour tournaments. Russell's first attempt was a Monday qualifier for the Fresh Express Classic in San Francisco; he finished birdie-eagle to make the main draw. He went on to finish second in the tournament, which earned him full status on the Web.com Tour for the rest of 2011. Two months later, he won his first Web.com tournament, finishing the year 12th on the money list, which gave him conditional status on the PGA Tour. Russell spent 2013 playing PGA Tour and Web.com events. At the Web.com Tour's Boise Open that year, he shot 59 in the second round, joining Annika Sorenstam as one of fewer than 20 players who have shot that score in competition.

Russell qualified for full PGA Tour exemption in 2014. One of the privileges that came with his PGA Tour card was membership at TPC Sawgrass, which is near his home in Jacksonville, Florida. Russell was excited. His neighbor Vijay Singh practiced at TPC Sawgrass. Russell started practicing with Vijay. As most people know, Vijay is famous for hitting thousands and thousands of balls on the practice range. Unfortunately, Russell started hitting too many balls and became overly fixated on his swing technique. His game fell apart, which is when he came back to us for additional coaching. Rather than focus on the quantity of balls hit, we turned his attention back to his balance, tempo, and tension. Soon he was in his groove again. "A lot of people think golf is all about the swing mechanics," says Russell. "But one of the biggest causes of bad shots is tension. When I go out with my buddies and I have no real tension in my body, I'll rarely hit a terrible shot. But in a tournament, when you're nervous and tight, it's amazing how you can hit a pretty awful shot. So I work a lot now on making tension-free swings in practice."

Balance, too, has become central to Russell's play. "I figure if I can complete my swing and stay in balance, the chance of hitting a good shot goes up significantly. I work on balance almost more than anything else. If I'm at home, I'll hit shots standing on one leg and hit shots with my eyes closed, just to set the feeling of my body in balance."

In May 2015, Russell's longtime swing teacher, Mike Flemming, died just before the Players Championship. Mike had been Russell's coach at the University of Jacksonville, and the loss was huge. He made the decision not to hire a new swing coach and to concentrate on using balance, tempo, and tension skills to manage his game, along with a few pre-swing check-ups such as posture and alignment. It wasn't an easy decision to make on the PGA Tour, where every player seems to have a personal swing coach and support team. Russell was clear about his decision, and why it would work. He was also confident he would succeed. "I'm never going to be the longest hitter," he told us, "but I could be the straightest driver of the ball the Tour has ever seen. I'm going to use my BTT skills to bring out the best in my own game—the Russell game."

In golf, the primary goal is to create and maintain a performance state in which you can play your best game. BTT is the bridge—an essential integration of your physical and technical skills. Each time you play, you must match your technical swing feels to your body, or physical state, for that day. Some days your body is tight, and other days it's more relaxed. Some days you feel sluggish, and other days you're amped up. These states are never fixed. Balance changes from shot to shot, hour to hour, day to day. Swing tempo changes with pressure or fatigue—or because of a tight lie or deep rough. Likewise, tension can show up in your shoulders or in your grip pressure, even in your jaw. We like to use the metaphor of "fresh produce" to describe these things: Lettuce and delicate vegetables go stale quickly, sometimes even before you have a chance to use them. Balance, tempo, and tension are the same. Your balance can be excellent in the morning, and off in the afternoon. Your tension level can be relaxed, but three holes later, your shoulders have tightened up. The human skills of balance, tempo, and tension awareness are the ability to listen and fine-tune these states accordingly.

BALANCE

BALANCE IS THE FIRST of the three elements we ask players to focus on. Humans access balance in our bodies in three ways: through our eyes, through the fluid in our ears, and through the proprioceptors or sensors in our body that give us information about where our limbs are in space. Our friend and colleague Greg Rose is co-founder of the Titleist Performance Institute in California, where he uses science-based conditioning to help players improve their performance. Greg explains that proprioception is the body's internal GPS system that allows us to navigate across any terrain and remain upright. Our proprioceptors are a highly sophisticated network of sensory receptors located in our muscles and joints that enable us to detect the basic motions and positional changes in our limbs and body during a golf swing. Being able to react and adjust to those motions and forces is critical to a consistent swing. Proprioceptors help us maintain a stable base, even if the factors involved in each shot are forever changing.

Simply put, proprioceptors are the keys to balance. They occur throughout your body, but you have an especially large number of them in your feet. If you are going to maintain good balance, your proprioceptors must be engaged—that is, turned on. This happens most effectively through movement or pressure changes. One of the easiest ways to train your proprioceptive system, Rose says, is to walk, hit balls, or practice barefoot. Going barefoot helps increase movement in the foot and ankle, and therefore helps stimulate the proprioceptors. If you take off your shoes and swing barefoot, you'll more clearly sense whether your weight is on the balls of your feet. Many of the players we coach have gained a better sense of balance, feel, tempo, and timing simply by hitting balls barefoot (though wearing just socks or standing on a towel works, too). We also encourage players to heighten their proprioceptive awareness by hitting with their feet together, on one foot, or with their eyes closed. Several of them even warm up before tournament rounds this way!

TEMPO

TEMPO IS ANOTHER KEY to good play. Swing tempo gives the player the ability to create the proper kinematic sequence, which is the natural motion the human body goes through in swinging a golf club. In the kinematic sequence of hitting a golf ball, your lower body moves first, followed by your upper body, then your arms, and finally your hands. The important thing is to know what sequence you have when you hit the ball well. The swings of golf's best ball-strikers might look entirely different (golf analyst David Feherty has described Jim Furyk's swing as looking like "an octopus falling out of a tree"), but what they have in common is an almost identical sequence that produces optimal impact as the club meets the ball.

This is why it's so important to develop body awareness. Some days you might be more energetic and alert, and so you're swinging at a faster speed to achieve optimal sequencing. Other days you might feel more tired or sluggish, and so you might need to slow down your tempo a notch to attain your best sequence. By practicing swinging the club and hitting the ball with different tempos—from 20 percent of your normal swing speed to 100 percent—you'll get better at making your swing and club work together. By learning to swing and putt with different tempos, you'll also learn to give yourself a variety of different shots. You might be able to hit a soft flop shot around the green much more effectively with a slower tempo. And likewise, if you're putting on very fast greens, you might choose to slow your putting tempo to 60 percent. If you're in very thick rough, you might increase your swing tempo. Practicing this variation will allow you to master these shots during a round.

A few summers ago, we spent a fascinating day coaching a group of golfers at Atlantic Golf Club in Bridgehampton, New York. We asked them what kinds of misses they tended to hit.

Jeff Goldberger, a 1-handicap, told us that when he misses a shot, he tends to hit a toe-iron or a toe-hook drive.

Lynn asked him, "Do you know what's technically causing you to do that?"

Jeff said, "Sure. On the drive, my hands are outracing my body. And my swing plane is off."

"So you're saying your swing is out of sequence," Lynn responded.

We suggested that Jeff try hitting shots at 75 percent and at 50 percent of his normal tempo. At 75 percent of his normal tempo, Jeff hit his shots as purely as he'd ever hit them. He realized that when he gets tense, his swing speeds up. By consciously slowing his swing, he counteracted his tendency to get too quick and returned his swing to optimal tempo *in the particular situation.*

"I see," Jeff said to us with a bit of wonder. "If I begin toe-hooking my shots, I know now that I can slow my swing tempo and that will reestablish proper sequence. That's pretty simple."

As we've mentioned, optimal performance comes when a player engages more of his or her right brain, the automatic, sensory-motor lobe. For a cerebral player like Jeff, focusing on balance, tempo, or tension releases his left brain and activates his right brain, allowing him to produce the shot he wants without cognitive interference.

Kevin Streelman, one of the PGA Tour pros we coach, is another highly analytic player—and one of the first on tour to use TrackMan to evaluate his swing. "I suffer from what I call the Duke Disease," Kevin admits with a laugh. "I went to Duke University, and I have a tendency to default to the rational, technical side of the game. I tend to lean on instructors quite a

bit, too, and I don't necessarily look to myself. I began search-
ing for another perspective because I got tired of doing video
analysis and the same three-foot drills every day."

Kevin came to us in 2005, and we started working on his
human skills, including balance, tempo, and tension. One day
we were on TPC Scottsdale's Stadium course with him. We
came to the 17th hole, which is a 332-yard drivable par-4 hole.
We asked Kevin to hit a drive with his usual tempo. The ball
stopped short of the green. We asked him to dial his tempo
back to 80 percent. He hit a second ball, and it rolled over the
green. Like Jeff Goldberger, he was amazed that *slower* tempo
often corrects faulty sequencing. In his case, it delivered more
distance. Which is why learning awareness and experiment-
ing on the course in the context of the game is so important.

TENSION

THE THIRD COMPONENT of the physical swing is tension. If
somewhere in your swing you've created unwanted tension,
it will interfere with your technique. For example, changing
your grip pressure during the swing has a direct influence on
what the clubface does. Change in grip pressure can make you
hit wild shots.

Similarly, if you get tight in your shoulders, your backswing
will shorten and all kinds of things can happen. This is why
it's important to become aware of how your body is reacting
to different situations on the course. Awareness enables you
to check your tension level—whether it's your grip pressure,
or upper body or shoulder tension. Then you can make adjustments as needed.

J.C. Anderson is a PGA professional who lives in St. Louis, where he teaches tour players as well as top amateur and high school golfers. J.C. told us, "There were times in the past that I would stand on the range with one of my players and be amazed at how beautifully he was hitting the ball. Then he would go out and shoot 85 in a tournament. I would scratch my head and think, *How do you hit the ball that well and still score an 85?* After working with VISION54, I know the answer. He may be relaxed on the range, but then he gets into competition and he tenses up. Tension ruins technique. For me, tension awareness, whether in your shoulders, arms, or grip, has become the key in my teaching and in my own play."

J.C. began using balance, tempo, and tension awareness in his own game after he attended a VISION54 program in December 2012. A month later he decided to play the PGA Winter Series in Florida. "I was pretty rusty at the first event because I hadn't had a chance to practice," he says. "My first tournament was the Senior Stroke Play Championship. All I focused on was my balance, tension, and tempo, particularly the tension in my shoulders and arms. I told myself before each shot: *Noodle arms, J.C. Noodle arms.* It worked! I won the tournament. Next thing you know, I won the PGA Cup and qualified for the PGA Championship that year. It was amazing."

Another story about tension awareness comes from our student Ken Kennedy, who is an architect in New York City and has played since he was a boy growing up in Australia. Ken was once a single-digit handicap; now he's 62 years old and has a busy career. Because he plays infrequently, his game was erratic. One day we did a few balance, tempo, and tension exercises with Ken before his round. For the first time, he noticed that he tended to tighten his grip on certain shots, particularly his drives, which used to slice or hook. He focused on relaxing his grip, and suddenly his shots were going long and straight, completely under his control. He told us the next time he played he shot 82—his best score in years.

We've become almost religious in our belief in the power of balance, tempo, and tension awareness. Especially for golfers who don't have much time to practice, these BTT skills can help you on almost every shot.

One of our favorite BTT stories goes back to Russell Knox. At the end of 2015, he was playing in a European Tour event in Malaysia. At the time, Russell hadn't won a PGA Tour event, and wasn't in the field for the upcoming WGC-HSBC Champions in Shanghai. But when another player dropped out of the WGC field, Russell suddenly got into the tournament from seventh reserve and third alternate.

Russell and his wife, Andrea, hurried over to the Chinese consulate and got visas. Unfortunately, his caddie had flown back to the U.S. with Russell's clubs, so he arrived at the tournament with nothing but the clothes on his back. He borrowed clubs for his practice rounds, and Andrea caddied for him until his caddie could fly to Shanghai. Even with these stressful conditions, Russell, a master of variability, stayed calm. During all four rounds, he focused solely on his balance, tempo, and tension. "It was a great week for me," he says. "When I made the turn on the back nine in the final round, I said to my caddie, 'I need to play great to win, but it doesn't need to be perfect.' Staying with my BTT was key to hitting the shots I needed."

Russell ended up beating Kevin Kisner by two strokes in

the final round for his first PGA Tour win. He became the only Scotsman ever to win a WGC event, and his ranking rose to No. 31 in the world, the first time he had broken into the top 50. The coolest thing was that the win earned him a spot in the 2016 Masters at Augusta. Although he missed the cut there, Russell went on to finish among the top 20 at the Players Championship and a few months later won the Travelers Championship for his career-best year. Not a bad season for BTT.

FOUNDATIONAL HUMAN SKILLS: BALANCE, TEMPO, AND TENSION

MANY GOLFERS COME TO US for help with their "mental skills." But afterward, they realize they've gained heightened awareness of their bodies and have new tools with which to manage themselves during play. One of our players said to us: "I came to VISION54 to get stronger mentally, and I came away having learned to be more physically aware and able to access my athletic ability."

Balance, tempo, and tension are what make your swing and stroke functional on the golf course. They make the swing come alive physically, not intellectually. With conditions always changing on the course, it's the players tuned into their BTT who can manage their swings and make adjustments to keep them fluid.

Play a few holes focusing on your balance; play a few holes focusing on your tempo; then play a few holes focusing on tension. Can you play an entire hole swinging with your feet together on each shot and finish in balance? Can you putt 18 greens on one leg and keep your balance?

A word of caution: When golfers practice BTT awareness on the course, they sometimes have a hard time staying with the exercises. One of the reasons is that while you're concentrating on the processes, you might lose awareness about the outcome of your shot. This is natural. Focusing on outcome draws you away from being present through your entire swing.

The following questions and explorations will lead you to a better awareness of your body and your swing on the course. When you can play an entire hole swinging with 50 percent tempo, you'll begin to appreciate how many more options you have for your game.

BALANCE, TEMPO, AND TENSION: QUESTIONS

- Can you hit five shots with your feet together and finish in balance?

- Can you hit three shots standing on your right foot and finish in balance? Can you do the same on your left foot?

- Can you make full swings with slow, medium, and fast tempo? What differences do you notice? Which feels best for you?

- Try out different grip pressures, and see what happens to your swing, your shot, and your ball flight. Can you find a favorite grip pressure, and keep it constant until the finish of your swing?

- How can you best use balance, tempo, and tension awareness to warm up for a round?

BALANCE, TEMPO, AND TENSION: ON-COURSE EXPLORATIONS

PLAY A NINE-HOLE PRACTICE ROUND, and do one of these explorations on each hole:

1. On one hole, hit your shots with your feet together, then chip and putt standing on only one leg (right or left). Finish in balance.

2. On one hole, hit your shots (including putts) with 50 percent of full tempo.

3. On one hole, hit your shots focused on keeping your shoulders relaxed.

4. On one hole, focus on feeling your feet during each swing. Where is your balance? Is it on the balls of your feet? On your heels?

5. On one hole, hit your shots with 75 percent of full tempo.

6. On one hole, play each shot focusing on feeling constant grip pressure.

7. On one hole, hit your shots with your eyes closed during the swing.

8. On one hole, make a practice swing before each shot standing on one foot. Finish your swing in balance.

9. On one hole, smile during your entire swing, all the way to the finish (smiling relaxes tension in your jaw).

Write down what you learned about yourself and your performance during these exercises.

PIA: THE SUPERFLUID KJELL ENHAGER

A COUPLE OF YEARS after I took a leave from the LPGA Tour, I was talking with Kjell Enhager, a fellow Swedish golf pro and one of the most creative thinkers I know. "I'm so frustrated," I said to Kjell. "These Swedish national team players I'm coaching, their thinking is so limited. They're always saying things like, 'We can't beat the Americans because they're too far ahead of us. We can't beat the Southern Europeans because their greens are better than ours. Our short games aren't as good as the Aussie players'. Our winters are too long.' All these excuses!"

I was looking for some input to jump-start my players. I knew I wanted something dynamic and related to golf, rather than traditional sports psychology. Kjell was my age. He was a longtime meditator and had studied at Maharishi University in Iowa. The first time we met for lunch in Stockholm, we talked for three hours. Kjell listened patiently to my thoughts and goals, and threw out some ideas for me to consider. He pointed out that our elite players hardly ever played tournaments on their home courses. He made the point that each of them had probably birdied every hole on a course they knew extremely well, which meant that it was theoretically possible to birdie every hole in one round. It was Kjell, not me, who came up with the idea of 54 as an aspirational score for golfers. Kjell was always the one with crazy ideas. I implemented them.

Kjell believed that to achieve better results, we need to work with both our conscious and our subconscious behaviors. He believed that players should focus on solutions rather than problems, and they should celebrate what they do well, rather than getting caught up in negative thought patterns. Kjell now works with individual athletes, sports teams, and companies, and gives very popular public lectures in Sweden. He loves to say, "The difference that makes the difference is you." This idea of focusing on our strengths and what enriches us is at the core of his work.

One of Kjell's most powerful ideas was "superfluidity." He borrowed the term from high-energy physics, where it is used to describe states in which matter behaves like a fluid with zero viscosity. Kjell wrote a novel, *Quantum Golf*, in which he describes superfluidity as the shift from a beta brainwave state (language-oriented and analytical) to alpha and brainwave states more conducive to higher motor skills. Alpha, theta, and other brainwave states are meditative, almost a form of self-hypnosis in which the golfer turns off the self-talking, outcome-obsessed left side of the brain and turns on the sensory-based, autopilot right side of the brain. "Superfluid" was a scientific term, but in the context of Kjell's novel, it was a fresh expression of the idea of the Shivas Irons style of golf mysticism that Michael Murphy wrote about in his novel *Golf in the Kingdom*.

Two decades later, with new performance-related neuroscience research to draw on, Lynn and I believe that there is nothing remotely mystical about performance states. We all have beta, alpha, theta, delta, and gamma brainwave capacities that influence how we play. Any golfer can learn about them and, with proper training, can discover how to access the ones that enhance performance. In our VISION54 vernacular, your optimal performance state takes place in the Play Box, a focused sensory state during which great golf swings happen.

The challenge is—and we've learned this from years of coaching—you can't enter this superfluid Play Box while *thinking* about your golf swing. Neuroscience tells us that we're not in the language part of the brain when we perform a task. We're in the sensory motor area. But if you're a typical golfer, you routinely engage with the language side of the brain when you're over the ball. *Okay, three-quarter backswing . . . gotta remember to turn the shoulders . . . keep your head down through impact.* You're giving yourself cognitive instructions instead of engaging your senses.

When we first experimented with this, we would explain it to our players, then send them out to try it on the course. They'd stand over the ball, thinking, *I'm not going to think about my swing . . . I'm present . . . I'm not talking to myself . . .* which, of course, was exactly what they were doing. So we cooked up some Play Box exercises to awaken the senses we use most in golf:

Hit three shots feeling your grip pressure.

Hit three shots and visualize a blue ball flying to the target.

Hit three shots while listening to the whoosh of the club or the sound of cars whizzing by on the highway.

The idea is simple and powerful. When you're present to something you can feel, hear, visualize, smell, or taste, you disengage the language center of the brain and engage the other brainwave states that control motor movement.

My eight-year coaching partnership with Kjell was incredibly generative and rewarding. Kjell remarked one day, "Only dead fish swim with the current." After that, our leadership group called ourselves The Living Fish Company.

Today, Kjell is famous for his work with athletes, actors, symphony orchestras, and corporate leaders. He's less famous for his mentoring of Pia Nilsson, but I can't describe my life and our VISION54 ideas without acknowledging Kjell's influence. He pushed, cajoled, and challenged me to widen my horizons and do things I had never dared to do, including the public speaking that I dreaded nearly as much as one of the young golfers I coached named Annika Sorenstam.

And did I mention that I'm a godmother to Kjell's son, August?

DURING THE ROUND

YOUR PERFORMANCE ROUTINE

THE AVERAGE ROUND OF GOLF can take anywhere from a delightful three-and-a-half hours to a painful five-plus hours. Unlike other sports, where the athlete is in near-constant motion, golf is performed in little bursts of action separated by lengthy intermissions. What's more, every shot requires a particular amount of thoughtful preparation. What's the wind doing? Where's the flag? What's the yardage? Is the bunker in play? Should I gamble or lay up?

It is impossible to focus intensely for four to five hours. Fortunately, golf allows you to take a break between shots and holes. In one round, you might walk, admire the landscape, feel the sun on your face, hit the good shots you intend, and talk with your friends. It is a sublime game.

On another day, you might ride in a cart huddled against rain and wind, fume over your mis-hits, agonize about whether your score is blowing up, and grow increasingly irritable at a playing partner. It is a volatile game.

On both the good day and the bad day, you still have to hit your next shot.

It's a fact that your body, mind, and emotions change during a round—and they all affect the way you perform. Your swing doesn't exist alone in cyberspace. How you think and feel can either improve your ability to hit a good shot or hurt it. Everything is interwoven. No one part of your golf game exists independently.

For most players, the time it takes to hit a golf shot is about 15 to 30 seconds, when all is going well. During that time we decide what kind of shot is required, step up to the ball, do some kind of final check, hit the ball, and evaluate the outcome. Note the natural sequence in this process. *We consider the conditions, decide on the shot, make a swing, and observe the outcome of the shot.*

Many golfers describe this shot-making process as their "routine." For most players, this series of actions takes place before the shot. A pre-shot routine gives a player information, in addition to the comfort of approaching each shot in a similar way. But a routine can also be a security blanket, or even a crutch. Do we really know what we are doing during our routines, internally and externally? What about the shot itself, and after the shot?

We've developed what we believe is a more comprehensive routine—what we call your *performance routine.* It's based on the idea that every shot has a future, a present, and a past. We've named the parts of this performance routine: Think Box, Play Box, and Memory Box. The Think Box is the period before the shot when you're evaluating the conditions, making a decision about the shot, and then shifting into a sensory state. It's characterized by analytic thought. The Play Box is the time and space over the ball in which you execute the shot. It's a sensory state—in which, for instance, you're feeling a low center of gravity or visualizing your ball flight. The Memory Box is your post-shot process. This is where you store positive shots and processes, and become neutral to negative shots. The three boxes are connected, and the flow between them is important. To recap: Think Box is about getting clear for a decision. Play Box is about being present, focused, and athletic. Memory Box is about creating confidence by managing what the brain stores as memory. Together they make up the complete, multidimensional experience of hitting the ball, from start to finish. Through on-course exploration, you will find your unique sequence and flow for all three boxes.

YOUR PERFORMANCE ROUTINE

THINK BOX		PLAY BOX	MEMORY BOX

One last point. We don't explain (or coach) the boxes in the linear order that they occur: Think Box, Play Box, and Memory Box. We start with the Play Box because you will need to understand the performance "feels," or states, that work best for you before you can select and commit to them. Make sense? Let's go to the boxes.

CHAPTER 4

THE SHOT:
PLAY BOX

I

N 2014, WE TRAVELED to Palo Alto, California, to do coaching sessions with Stanford University's women's and men's golf teams. Anne Walker, the coach of the women's team, asked if we might have some additional time to work with a Stanford professor who is one of the teams' strongest supporters. The person turned out to be former secretary of state Condoleezza Rice. Condoleezza teaches in Stanford's political science department as well as the Hoover School of Public Policy and the Graduate School of Business. She's a 13-handicapper, has served on committees of the United States Golf Association, and is one of the few women members of Augusta National Golf Club.

We've coached many high-achieving golfers over the years—lawyers, scientists, surgeons, musicians, and CEOs—so we had a good idea of what to expect with Condoleezza, and planned a little icebreaker to begin our time together. When she met us at the Stanford golf range, we'd written on the whiteboard: WELCOME TO YOUR BRAINIAC54 TRAINING.

First we gave a short overview of VISION54 and the elements we believe go into playing golf: Physical, Technical, Mental, Emotional, Social, and Spirit of the Game. We talked about how each of these factors—in addition to technique—influences your swing and your game. It was fun to watch Condi's *Aha!* moments as she took it all in. She told us that everywhere she goes to play, somebody has a swing tip for her. "Sometimes I have so many things going on in my head that when I'm about to swing the club, I can't even focus," she said with a rueful laugh.

Condoleezza is like many of us today. Our jobs and busy lives require that we spend most of our waking time in our heads. This tendency transfers to the golf course, too, which means that most of us overthink our golf games—or at least think in the wrong places. To play good golf, you need to balance thinking and sensory awareness. If one is too strong, you need to rebalance them. We drew a big circle on the board with the words "Play Box" inside. Beside it, we drew a much smaller circle with the words "Think Box." We said to her, "Condi, your Play Box needs to get much bigger, and your Think Box needs to get much smaller."

Very simply, the Play Box is golf's moment of truth. On one level, it's the three-dimensional space where you actually swing the club. On another level, it's your interior state that creates the conditions for a good swing. It takes 1.7 seconds to swing the club. From stepping into the shot to the finish of the swing, the Play Box should take from four to nine seconds. That's not very long, which is why this window is so important. Peter Saika, a Canadian golfer and reader of our books, puts it this way: "I think of the swing like a Q-Tip," he says. "There's so much attention focused on the ends—that is, where the club starts and where the ball ends up—that everybody glosses over the middle. The problem is, when you put too much focus on the end points, you usually have no idea how you got there."

We couldn't agree more.

This is why we wanted Condoleezza to focus on her Play Box. Here, in the middle of the Q-Tip, the Play Box is the space for pure sensory awareness. What do we mean by sensory awareness? We mean awareness related to the five senses: seeing, touching, hearing, tasting, and smelling. Remember, these senses live in the right side of the brain. No matter what kind of performance you're engaged in, you will generate optimal motor movements through your right, or sensory, brain. For a "left"-brain person like Condoleezza, learning to access sensory "feel" in the Play Box is a new—and critical—skill.

It's why we put so much emphasis on developing awareness of balance, tension, and tempo. Accessing these three physical states will move you away from cognitive thinking. Our friend Dr. Debbie Crews of Arizona State University studies golfers' brainwaves by attaching electrodes to their scalps and recording the electrical activity of their brains while they play. She puts it this way: "The Think Box is where you make your decisions about your shots. Once your intention is set, you move your focus to achieving your intention. As you get closer to actually swinging the club, you want to activate more 'feel' and less 'thinking.' The moment just before you move the club is most predictive of your result. For the best golfers, the left side of the brain quiets down tremendously as they're about to start the swing, and the right side of the brain becomes more active. I call this synergy, where the conscious and unconscious parts of the brain come into balance."

One of our VISION54 students is a renowned neurosurgeon who works at Washington University in St. Louis. He described this synergy in his own way: "Let me tell you what happens when I do a neurosurgical procedure. The surgical movements and maneuvers occur in a delicate sequence. I concentrate on the goal of the surgical movement, not the mechanics of the movement. My knowledge base and the concept of the surgery are set long before the procedure is performed. Having formed a plan and a goal for the surgery, I need to let my intuition take over to visualize and achieve the surgical objective. This involves the 'sensory' parts of my brain, not the language or strictly cognitive brain networks. Essentially, I'm in my Play Box during the surgery."

Debbie Crews reminds us that the left brain, the language and decision center, comprises only about 5 to 10 percent of our brain power. "The right brain is about 90 to 95 percent of our brain power," she says. "Our right brain allows us to perform motor movements more successfully, because the subconscious is like a supercomputer. The left-side language center gets everything organized, but it can't run motor movement efficiently. It takes 450 milliseconds to complete the swing, from the top into impact. The club is traveling at 50 mph to more than 100 mph, and so the left brain can't do much with that. It just isn't able to send information to our muscles fast enough."

This is why players who clutter their brains with swing thoughts during their strokes often don't make many good swings while playing. *I'm stuck. Better throw my hands at the ball. Those tree limbs on the right side of the fairway are sticking out. I need to hit the ball to the left.* Many of us aren't even aware that we're thinking these thoughts. We don't perceive our interior monologue as separate from the part of the brain that has agency over performance. We stay stuck on the left side of our brains, and in response, our bodies essentially short-circuit.

Accessing a "feel" state helps you shift into that right side of the brain. "Our data shows that the two variables that help this process are feel and target," Debbie says. "'Feel' is a product of the right brain, whether it's sensing a low center of gravity in your body or feeling the state of getting to your left side in your finish. 'Target' is also right brain; your focus is on a visual image, maybe the flag or your aiming point in the fairway. Activating a target focus is not something you can order your brain to do as a sequence or set of events."

The greatest golfers of all time probably never called the state in which they hit the ball the "Play Box," but they implicitly understood the very natural, sensory aspect of the golf swing. Jack Nicklaus wrote in his book *Golf My Way* that he *saw* every shot in its entirety before he started his swing, suggesting that he operated out of a heightened visual sense. Sam Snead liked to practice barefoot; he wanted to *feel* the ground under his feet, and he said he swung the club to an internal waltz rhythm (that is, tempo). Arnold Palmer threw his entire body into the shot. He lived for the physical sensation of the pure strike. Each of them understood the unique sensory "feel" necessary to achieve peak performance. Jack Nicklaus was a relatively slow player standing over the ball, especially on putts. Lynn has talked with Jack's longtime caddie, Angelo Argea, who was on his bag for more than 20 years. He recalled how before Jack would putt, he would visualize every revolution of the ball toward the hole. He would see it drop into the cup, and then visually reverse the ball's motion all the way back to his putterface. Jack wasn't having a debate about his line with himself. He was waiting for the picture of the shot to complete itself. He wouldn't step up to the ball until that picture was crystal clear.

Tiger Woods's version of his "Play Box" was more tactile. When he played well, he would say, "I felt the shots in my hands." One year at the Masters he told reporters, "I can feel the target in my hands." The more competitive a match became, the more he was able to heighten his ability to access his senses.

Like Nicklaus, Annika Sorenstam always visualized her shot standing behind the ball and looking toward her target. She described feeling the shot in her gut. The moment she felt it, she would step up to the ball and hit. Annika was described as a fast player; she was fast because she didn't want to lose the sensory feeling she was accessing in her Play Box.

Ai Miyazato, an LPGA Tour player from Japan whom we coach, experiences her Play Box feeling as a low center of gravity in her abdomen or a smooth tempo. The famously unorthodox Canadian golfer Moe Norman said he could taste a good shot. LPGA Tour golfer Brittany Lincicome finds a visual connection to her target, whether it's the flag, a tree, or a bunker in the fairway. "If I'm going for the pin, I see that pin over and over in my brain before I hit," she says.

We suggested to Condoleezza that she try different Play Box sensory "feels" as she hit shots on the range. She visualized her ball flight as a blue trajectory line, and she experimented with grip pressures and tried sensing her swing at 75 percent of her normal tempo. In addition, she imprinted a target in her brain, created relaxation in her shoulders, and paid attention to the sound of the club and ball at impact. She tried counting her breaths and putting her hand on her heart to feel her heartbeats. All of these sensory "feelings" helped shift her focus away from the left side of her brain.

We'll be honest: Learning which sensory awarenesses work for you in your Play Box takes practice. You need to initiate your "feel" for every shot. You can never go on automatic. Fortunately, Condoleezza had been a competitive figure skater when she was young, so she understood the idea of the performance state. "I knew about visualization from skating," she says. "Before a competition, I would always visualize myself going through my program. But I had never really thought about it in golf. Did I see the shot? Did I hear the shot? Did I 'feel' the shot in my feet? Using my senses in golf was completely new."

Condi is also a concert-level pianist, and she has strong hands. When she was a child, her piano teacher would say to her, "Condi, you don't have to hammer the keys. Don't put so much muscle into playing." She said she realized she had a tendency to do the same thing with the golf club, so focusing on a constant, light grip pressure helps her find a calmer, more physical state.

Staying present to a sensory "feel" for the entire duration of her shot was also a new idea. "In figure skating, your performance is only a three-and-a-half-minute burst of energy, but you have to be present the entire time—or you'll end up on your rear end," she says. "Taking that feeling of being in the present, and not letting your mind wander, has been an important thing for me to learn for my golf game.

"I'm one of the fastest players on earth," she adds, laughing. "I learned to play when I was secretary of state, so I never had much time. When I got the chance to play, I was running out onto the course to try and catch a few holes somewhere before dark. One thing I'm trying to do is to use the sensory state to slow myself down. I tell myself, *Just be in the present*. When I've decided what club to use and what shot to hit, I stand over the ball, clear my mind, and connect my energy to the target. I've found this special moment now, and I love the idea of being present."

We've coached opera singers and professional musicians before, but Condi helped make the similarities between golf and music more clear. "Like swinging a golf club, playing the piano is a very complicated set of movements," she explains. "People think of making music as artistic, but it's extremely physical. You've got to make big leaps across the keyboard with your fingers at exactly the right moments. Striking the right key at the right time takes a lot of coordination and a lot of focus."

She told us about the time she was invited to perform Schumann's Piano Concerto in A Minor with the Omaha Symphony a few years ago. "I hadn't played with an orchestra since I was 19 years old, and I realized I'd have to play without the score because there was no page-turner available. A friend who's an experienced pianist told me, 'Learn the piece by slowing down to the point where every movement is completely isolated. If you do that, you'll know the piece.'"

Several famous golfers, including Ben Hogan, have used a similar idea, practicing tai chi swings, which are extremely slow repetitions of the full swing. (You can look up videos of Ben Hogan's slow-motion practice routine on YouTube.) We do this in our programs, too. The VISION54 record for one complete swing in extremely slow motion is five minutes and 15 seconds. Condoleezza decided to apply the tai chi method to her own golf swing. "I use this in my own practice now when I'm working on my technique," she says. "When I go out onto the course, I put it all together."

After exploration, Condi chose balance, breathing, and grip pressure as her Play Box sensory "feels." "It's a very simple thing to make sure you're swinging in balance," she says. "I take a practice swing before my shot with my feet together, which gives me a super-centered feeling over the ball." She also focused on maintaining the feel through the end of her swing and not stopping it at impact.

Condoleezza can now rely on her sensory awareness skills to get herself out of trouble. "I was playing in Korea not long ago," she says. "I was there to give a speech, and my host is an avid golfer, so he wanted to play. I don't know why—maybe it was the environment or I was tired—but I couldn't hit the ball straight for the first four holes. I was spraying it all over the place. So I stopped and said to myself, *Okay, you're not present over your shots.* I took a moment just to pause, put my feet together, and feel *balance, balance, balance.* I started hitting the ball much better. So I've seen how the Play Box 'feel' can help you make corrections in the middle of a round. I also like to take a few deep breaths as I approach the ball. Those are my go-to states."

After one recent coaching session with Condi, she said something we loved. "If people can get away from all that technical stuff—*Are my hands high enough? Am I coming from the inside?*—the game becomes more enjoyable. I know I still have to do technical maintenance work on my swing, but using these human skills makes golf feel more like a sport. And that's more fun."

We've seen how a reliable Play Box "feel" can help alleviate anxiety on the course, too. Under pressure, which each person experiences differently on the course—a tight fairway, hitting over water, leading a tournament into the final few holes, etc.—the left side of the brain will attempt to take over, which could mean trouble. After determining which Play Box "feels" work for you, the next stage of mastery is to work on deepening those sensations, so you can rely on them when a match is on the line or you're putting to win a tournament.

In 2016, we began working with Ariya Jutanugarn, the astonishingly talented young player from Thailand. Ariya (whose nickname is May) was a phenom at a young age, and qualified for the Honda LPGA Thailand tournament when she was just 11, making her the youngest player ever to qualify for an LPGA Tour event. Over the next few years, she exhibited a powerful game, but she also suffered some epic meltdowns. In 2013, when she was 17, May had a two-shot lead heading into the final hole of the Honda LPGA Thailand. With her countrymen and -women watching, and on the verge of becoming the first Thai player to win an LPGA tournament, May triple-bogeyed the 18th hole to lose by one stroke to Inbee Park.

Her collapse occurred in front of her entire nation, which is a tough thing for a 17-year-old. She managed to climb to No. 15 in the Rolex Women's World Rankings that year, but then she tore the labrum in her shoulder. Even though Ariya earned her LPGA Tour card in 2014, she struggled. She began to doubt her shots, including her drive, once the best shot in her arsenal. "I knew the problem wasn't my swing," she explains. "It was nothing with my golf game—only my brain. I got to the point where I was scared to hit the ball. I was scared to miss cuts in a tournament. I kept thinking about all the bad things that could happen. Everything got worse and worse. I knew that if I kept on with the same thing, I wasn't going to win. So I tried to find help."

That's when Ariya's agent called us.

Early in 2016, we spent four days with Ariya and her sister Moriya, who also plays on the LPGA Tour. We taught them about the performance routine—Think Box, Play Box, and Memory Box. "It made very much sense to me," says Ariya. "Before, I didn't call this part of my routine Think Box or this part Play Box. It was all mixed up together."

Ariya had always been a natural ball-striker. She had managed to play well enough, even though she lacked commitment and tended to be unfocused during her shots. We knew that her natural talent could take her only so far.

During a practice round before an LPGA tournament in San Francisco, we did an on-course exercise with Ariya and Moriya. They explored different ways of getting present with their senses before stepping into their Play Boxes. On one hole, they each practiced "seeing" the ball flight in a bright color. On another hole, they "felt" the shot in their guts; on another, they relaxed their shoulders; and on another, they stated their decisions out loud to reinforce their commitment to the shot. On one hole, we asked them to access a "feeling" of happiness before their shots. It resonated immediately with Ariya. She began using the "happy feeling" regularly for her Play Box, which she would trigger by smiling as she approached her ball. (Many people have now commented on Ariya's "smile"; what they may not know is that it's the secret to her Play Box.)

"It didn't come right away," Ariya says. "I needed to practice it. At first, when I go to my Play Box, I'm still thinking about something else. But then I start to know what 'feeling' makes me comfortable to hit the ball. Suddenly I'm not scared. This helps me more every day."

In April 2016, Ariya played in the ANA Inspiration in Rancho Mirage, California, the LPGA Tour's first major of the year. On Sunday, she had a two-shot lead over World No. 1 Lydia Ko after the 15th hole. Everything looked sharp, until she made three consecutive bogeys, including a snap-hook tee shot into the water on the 18th hole to lose by two strokes.

Ariya cried afterward, but this time she wasn't devastated. We talked with her about what we had observed during those last three holes. All players react differently to pressure. Some over-read putts. Others get too slow or too fast with their swings. Ariya's tempo got way too fast during her last three holes. We shared with her that she looked tense in her shoulders and around her mouth. Her smile looked forced. She wasn't taking deep breaths.

"I *thought* I had a good Play Box," she said later. "It was working fine until I got really nervous. Then it didn't work anymore. Pia and Lynn told me afterward, 'When you are nervous and excited, you may need a deeper Play Box "feel" or sensory state to help you through. If your tendency is to swing too fast under pressure, you may need to "feel" 60 percent of full tempo and take long exhales before you swing. Or you may need to change your Play Box "feel" altogether.' So I practiced some more. Now I take a *really* deep breath when I move from Think Box to Play Box at important moments. I feel *extra happy* and I tell myself, *I love this shot* before I go to my Play Box. That feeling makes me smile. It works."

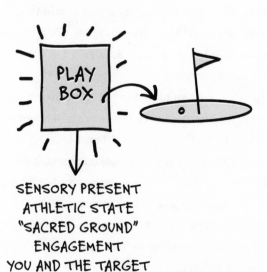

SENSORY PRESENT
ATHLETIC STATE
"SACRED GROUND"
ENGAGEMENT
YOU AND THE TARGET

We're very proud of Ariya. Using her stronger sensory skills, she went on an impressive stretch the rest of 2016. She won the Yokahama Tire Classic. The following week, she won the LPGA Kingsmill Championship, followed by the Volvik Championship the next week, where she pulled away from the field by five strokes on the back nine. Those three consecutive wins put Ariya into some exclusive company in the LPGA history book. Only four players—Mickey Wright, Kathy Whitworth, Annika Sorenstam, and Lorena Ochoa—had won four tournaments in a row on Tour. Ariya, with three consecutive victories, came just one shy of that mark.

"I'm different now," she says. "I'm interested and happy about every shot, no matter if it's a good or a bad shot. Think Box and Play Box have given me a way to play, and tools to use, so that I'm confident I can reach my potential. They help me see golf as a very big exploration rather than a fear."

YOUR PERFORMANCE ROUTINE: PLAY BOX

AFTER MANY YEARS of teaching and coaching, the general observation we have about golfers—professional and amateur—is that they are "over-present" to elements of the game such as practice, technique, and results. They spend time on the range memorizing their swing thoughts, and focusing on their equipment, scores, handicaps, tournament wins, and losses. But they are "under-present" when they're actually hitting a golf shot. Bringing the Play Box to the course is one of the most important skills a golfer can add to his or her game.

When we ask players to stay focused on a "feel" such as grip pressure through their entire swing on the practice range, they're pretty good at it. But when we take them onto the course, and ask them to stay present to the "feel" until the end of their swing, it's not so easy. When they get onto the course, their attention naturally shifts to the outcome of the shot— that is, where the ball landed. They forget about that Play Box "feel." Understanding that you haven't stayed with your shot until the end of the swing is something you can only see in the context of the game. Only on the course can you see your true patterns that emerge under pressure—and how the Play Box sensory states can help them.

We don't want to overcomplicate the Play Box. It's a simple, natural state that we automatically access in most reactive sports. You make a decision when you throw or kick a ball, then you do it instinctively. Golfers, however, can have a hard time *finding* that Play Box, which is why we recommend different sensory options. Focusing on "feeling" grip pressure, or "seeing" your ball flight, makes it easier to be present to something specific.

Your ultimate goal is to find several Play Box "feels" to stay with through your entire swing—on the golf course. Like Ariya, you might find you need different "feels" for different shots, different clubs, and different situations. Explore various sensory states, and build a routine that includes a repertoire of good, deep Play Box "feels" that you can rely on for your entire round.

PLAY BOX: QUESTIONS

- How well can you keep a Play Box sensation until the very end of your swing?

- How deeply can you focus in your Play Box? (When it's very deep, you won't get distracted or bothered by things around you.)

- How short, while still being effective, can you keep your Play Box?

PLAY BOX: ON-COURSE EXPLORATION

PLAY NINE HOLES, and on each hole, explore one of these Play Box "feels" during your swings.

1. On one hole, choose to see the ball flight or the target in your mind's eye.

2. On one hole, either feel constant grip pressure or softness in your shoulders.

3. On one hole, listen for the sound of impact or hum a song.

4. On one hole, choose your Play Box awareness, and hold it until the ball lands and stops rolling.

5. On one hole, close your eyes and experience a strong Play Box "feel" before stepping into the shot.

6. On one hole, play with a general Play Box sensation of feeling free and athletic during each swing.

7. On one hole, feel 100-percent connection to your target.

8. On one hole, use one Play Box sensation for your back-swing, and a different "feel" for your forward swing. (For example, see your ball flight in yellow on your backswing,

and switch to seeing the ball flight in blue on your forward swing. Or "feel" your back leg in your backswing, and your front leg in your forward swing.)

9. On one hole, go twice as deep with your sensory focus and engagement in the Play Box for each swing.

SEVERAL YEARS AGO, Pia and I heard about a psychologist who seemed to share our VISION54 philosophy. Carol Dweck is a professor at Stanford University and the author of a book titled *Mindset: The New Psychology of Success.* She studies people's beliefs about intelligence, and how those beliefs influence the way we learn. Generally, Carol characterizes people's theories about mental ability in two ways. The first is a fixed mind-set, in which one believes their intelligence and aptitudes are allotted at birth and set in stone. Fixed-mind-set individuals tend to see failure as a negative judgment on their innate abilities. The second theory is a growth mind-set. People with growth mind-sets believe success comes from learning, training, and practice, and that aptitude and intelligence can be enhanced through hard work. Growth-mind-set people see their own agency in the world, engage difficult challenges with openness and optimism, and treat failure as an impetus to learn more and try harder. They believe that a person's true potential is unknown, and unknowable.

We were fortunate to meet Carol at Stanford while we were coaching the Stanford men's and women's golf teams. We had a fascinating two-hour lunch with her, where she made the point that all of us have some fixed mind-sets—and they can come and go in different areas of our lives. Awareness is the key; when you become aware of your fixed mind-set and behavior, you have the ability to make a shift.

Neuroscience research supports this. Neuroplasticity is the brain's own growth mind-set. With effort and experimentation, we are continually creating new neural pathways in our brains. The fixed mind-set says, "Look smart, never look bad." The growth mind-set says, "You may fail before you succeed. Learn as much as you can."

Carol believes that the way parents teach their children can often lead to them developing fixed or growth mind-sets. Telling children "You're the best" or "You're great" is praising them for innate talent. More helpful is accentuating and rewarding effort, not outcomes. She tells her students on the first day of class, "If you focus only on your grade, you may miss the opportunity to learn."

I could have been one of Carol's case studies. As a young golfer, I reached the semifinals of the 1974 New York State Junior Championship. It was my first big tournament, and I was having a lot of fun, but my parents and their friends became totally fixated on my winning. "You played like a champion, Lynn! You're definitely going to get a college golf scholarship!" Just like that, I switched from a growth mind-set (*I'm having fun, let's see where this takes me*) to a fixed mind-set (*I have to play well or my parents will be unhappy and I won't get a scholarship*). From that day, I constantly measured myself against other girls my age and my best performances—neither of which allowed me to take enough risks or open up to new ways of learning how to play golf. I boxed myself into a fixed mind-set until much later in life.

One day during a VISION54 school, we asked a student to stop making practice swings before her shots, so that she could simplify her pre-shot routine. We were on a par-3 hole with a tee shot over water, and she promptly chunked her 7-iron into the pond. She turned to us and said angrily, "See? That didn't work." But she missed the point. There was a lot to learn from her chunked 7-iron shot. *Did I have tension in my upper body? How was my tempo? Did I lose focus in my Play Box before I hit the ball? Did I let past memories of par 3s take over?* Progress occurs even when the outcome is failure.

We believe that Carol's book validates our "human skills" approach to golf. The growth mind-set says that mistakes can help us learn. When golfers' mind-sets get too fixated on their scores or how they want a shot to turn out, they lose their capacity for learning. That's why we encourage golfers to spend more time learning on the course rather than the range. Failure and success, in the context of how we really play the game, is the best way to improve.

Annika Sorenstam had a natural growth mind-set. When she first went to LPGA Tour Qualifying School in 1992, she failed to earn her full Tour card, earning a conditional one instead. That meant she would have to Monday-qualify each week to get into most tournaments—a formidable challenge. Pia was at the Qualifying School that week. Annika had done everything she set out to do, yet the outcome didn't happen. Pia was on the same plane with Annika when she flew back to Sweden. She told Pia, "I'm fine. I'm going to have the opportunity to play Monday qualifying rounds every week. Sixty players will be competing for two spots, so I'll get even more experience playing under pressure. I'll either qualify and get to play the tournament, or I'll miss and have the week to practice—which will make me even stronger in the future." She was practicing a growth mind-set.

While meeting with Carol, we were struck by her fondness for the word "yet." As in: *You haven't mastered your emotions—yet.* Or: *You haven't birdied that difficult third hole—yet.* Carol believes that "yet" is one of the most powerful words we can add to our vocabularies. "Yet" establishes the growth mind-set. Commit, be tenacious, but also be open to failure and learning. Whatever skill or goal you haven't perfected or reached *yet* is still achievable.

Pia and I have tested our VISION54 methods against Carol's fixed- and growth-mind-set frames. We're happy to report VISION54 lives in the growth-mind-set world. We don't want you to fixate on outcomes. We want you to develop the awareness that will help you learn about your own processes and performance states—what works and what doesn't. What did you learn about yourself today? How are you better than yesterday? What will you do differently tomorrow? It's your game. It's your journey. Failure can be an opportunity to learn—if you allow it.

CHAPTER 5

BEFORE THE SHOT:
THINK BOX

WHEN WE STARTED coaching Condoleezza Rice, we asked her about her personal traits, and which ones had most contributed to her professional success. Condi pointed to her ability to synthesize information quickly and efficiently. "I'm fast in everything I do, especially thinking," she said.

Although both Play Box and Think Box are important to the performance routine, most of us are more comfortable in the Think Box, because it occupies the language portion of our brain. This is where you make decisions about your shots before you hit them. There are three things you need to do in the Think Box. You need to select the shot you're going to hit. You need to choose and commit to the sensory state that you'll use in your Play Box. And you need to be present to that sensory state you've chosen before you step into the Play Box.

The first task is gathering facts about your upcoming shot: Analyze the distance, decide on your target, pick the type of shot you want to hit, and which club you're going to use. Here's a caveat: In golf, there's always more than one right decision, so the clarity of your choice matters. Even more important than your decision is your commitment to it.

It's also critical to understand that we have more than one "brain." Yes, there's the one in our skull that deals with logic, creativity, emotions, and physical sensations, but scientific research has shown that we also have a "gut" brain and a "heart" brain. The gut brain is a separate nervous system in the gut lining (called the Enteric Nervous System or ENS) that's so complex and sensitive that it has been called our "second" brain. First discovered in the early 1900s, it comprises 500 million neurons that stretch from the esophagus to the anus. The gut brain mainly controls digestion, but it's also the transmitter for our most basic instincts—danger and pleasure. Thus, we describe our gut-brain responses like: "I had a gut feeling I shouldn't hit that shot," or "I got butterflies in my stomach when I met him/her."

The heart brain is now acknowledged to be our third brain. Besides its physiological function of pumping blood to every part of the body, the heart also responds to higher-order emotions such as happiness, gratitude, and love, and lower-order emotions such as anxiety, frustration, and anger. These emotions either positively or negatively affect something called "heart-rate variability," which is the time between heartbeats and the rate of those beats. Heart-rate variability, in turn, can affect the efficiency of our motor skills—that is, how we swing the golf club. (We'll get to this later, but this is another reason why it's important to be able to control our reactions and emotions on the course.) The three brains—our head's brain, gut's brain, and heart's brain—are connected by the longest nerve in the body, which is called the vagus nerve. The vagus nerve starts in the skull and reaches down along the spine through the heart into the gut, relaying information back and forth among your three brains.

Many people aren't aware they have a gut brain or a heart brain, and don't know that these brains influence athletic performance. Golfers spend most of their cognitive time with their head's "brain" processing data about yardage, wind, and swing thoughts. Awareness and management of your other brains might be the next frontier of performance. The science is still in an early stage.

As you prepare for your shot in the Think Box, the first thing you want to do is check your facts. What is the wind doing? What's your lie? What type of shot do you want to hit, and with which club? Where do you stand in your match or score? Once you've made your decisions, check in with your gut, and make sure it's congruent with your brain. If your mental side says the shot is an 8-iron but your gut says it's a 7-iron, consider the reasoning for both before making a decision you can trust. You might have played the same hole yesterday and successfully used an 8-iron, but today your gut knows that you're tired, and so you need one more club. So take in the facts, listen to your gut, and make sure your gut brain is on the same page.

In August 2016, PGA Tour player Russell Knox needed to make a 12-foot putt on the 18th green at the Travelers Championship to win the tournament. "I'd been reading putts for myself all day," he says, "but there were a few that I'd asked my caddie to read for me, and I didn't make those."

On the final putt, Russell again started to ask his caddie the read. He recalls, "He began to tell me and I suddenly said, 'Hold up. I don't want to hear it.' It was really important for me to trust my gut and take ownership of the decision."

Russell sank the putt, made par, and won his second PGA Tournament by one stroke.

We want to make one important point about facts. There's compelling research on "information fatigue and overload." We live in the Internet age, where we're overloaded with information all the time. Often we're presented with so much data that we can't pull the trigger. We've also become interested in research on an area called decision fatigue. If you keep gathering more and more information, your brain gets exhausted before you even make the decision. The simpler you can keep your process, the better. Consider how much information you really need on the golf course. Do you really need to look in your yardage book, check your Garmin watch, or ask your playing partners about the break of the putt? Do you really need to take one more look at the angle of your shot, and make four more practice swings to check your technique? How much information do you really *need* versus how much information do you *want*? Don't clutter your Think Box with too much data.

Another pattern we've noticed in players on the course is the tendency to force decisions. They're either not listening to their gut or they're trying to make a decision they think is right. "But I'm *supposed* to hit this club from this distance." Psychological research shows our decisions are constantly being influenced by unconscious biases, projections, and irrationalities. This is why we need to practice on the course. These patterns show up in the context of the real game. They don't show up on the practice range.

Not surprisingly, people who spend their waking hours in analytic work tend to overemphasize their Think Boxes. According to Dr. Debbie Crews, a player needs to "close the door" on the thinking part of their shot. "The problem is that players often don't know when they're finished," she says. "They keep thinking and thinking, so when they step into their Play Box, they're still in the cognitive or beta wave part of their brain, which is not the performance state. Don't make a big deal of stopping your thinking process," says Debbie. "Just finish, commit to the shot, and trust your decision."

After making your decision about your shot, the second stage of the Think Box is selecting which sensory state you'll use in your Play Box. Condoleezza settled on light grip pressure, breathing, or staying present in the moment—depending on her situation.

One player who we find fascinating to watch shift from his Think Box to his Play Box is PGA Tour pro Jason Day. Jason makes his decision about his shot. Then he stands behind the ball and closes his eyes, as if he's entering a deeply meditative state. His eyelids flutter. He explained in an article in *The Wall Street Journal* that he is visualizing his shot, not only its length and direction, but the shape of its trajectory through the air all the way to the target. He asks himself a question, such as, "What does a low, left-to-right 7-iron shot look like?" Then he lets his brain show him the answer. "I struggled to see it when I had my eyes open," he said, "but when I closed my eyes, I could see everything." Jason won't step up to the ball until he's totally present to the picture and feeling he wants.

Amy Lane, our student in New York, says she selects two Play Box feels: a low center of gravity in her body and a focus on holding her finish for an extra second or two at the end of her swing. "I accentuate the feeling that I've gotten to my left side," she says. "The minute I have that feeling, I'm ready to step into my Play Box."

Amy was activating the third stage of the Think Box, something we call "bridging." This is a subtle move, and can be tricky, because selecting the state isn't the same as activating it. Selecting it is only selecting it with your left brain. You need to activate the state and feel it in your body before you step into your Play Box. Initiating it before you move into the Play Box calms the language center, and begins the shift to the right side of the brain. It doesn't happen automatically. That's why LPGA pro Ariya Jutanugarn now takes one long inhale, then exhales and smiles before moving into her Play Box. She is bridging into her sensory state. Other players shrug their shoulders to initiate a feeling of relaxation, or see the target strongly in their mind's eye. They are triggering a deeper focus state as they enter their Play Box.

For Condoleezza Rice, activating her sensory state earlier in her pre-shot routine was critical to becoming more present. Condi says it enables her to "transport"—a word we love.

If you're not fully clear about your decision, or haven't fully committed to your Play Box state, step away from the ball and start over. It's perfectly acceptable to rethink a shot, as long as you check the decision with your gut again. When you get the "go" signal from your gut, step into your Play Box and hit the ball.

For many of our students, especially those who have been playing golf their whole lives, the Think Box and Play Box are clarifying concepts that work immediately. We saw this with teaching pro J.C. Anderson, whose Play Box feel is "noodle arms," a tactile feeling that his arms were as relaxed as wet noodles. Ariya Jutanugarn initiates her bridge to her Play Box with her smile; Condi does it with breathing and light grip pressure.

Alexandra "A.K." Frazier is a top amateur player from Philadelphia who competes in national USGA tournaments. A.K. first learned about Think Box and Play Box while reading our book *Every Shot Must Have a Purpose* on a plane going to Florida to play in the Doherty Women's Amateur Tournament. "I thought, *Hey, I'm going to try this. Why not?*" she says.

"I hadn't held a club since September, and here it was January," she recalls. "I didn't know about synchronizing the two parts of the brain, or that we perform best in the alpha/theta brainwave state. I just thought there might be something to this. I was excited about a new aspect of looking at the game. I found that Think Box and Play Box can help take care of almost everything, from playing through nerves to not letting distractions enter your head while you're trying to swing the golf club."

A.K. finished the tournament as co-medalist.

Think Box and Play Box helped another one of our students, Janet Daniels, overcome her fear of competing. On an evening before a Ladies Day or tournament at her club, Janet used to become paralyzed with anxiety. Finally her husband said, "Janet, this is really not good for you. You have to find another way to deal with this." Janet came to our VISION54 program and learned about Think Box and Play Box. She says they became tools that helped her overcome anxiety before a round, and frustration and anger on the course. "Now I concentrate on Think Box and Play Box. That's all. I decide on my shot, I commit to my Play Box feel, and I stay with it through my swing. With that feeling of presence, my anxiety and fear completely disappeared. If a shot goes awry, I think about whether I truly committed to the shot or to my Play Box feel. If not, I know I need to deepen my state. I sleep well before tournaments now. I don't panic for an hour before I tee off. I don't get to the practice range super early. I know I have my Think Box and Play Box routines. They're the only tools I need, and they'll take care of me."

Amy Lane regularly practices committing to a sensory state on the golf course, rather than the practice range. During a clinic we did with Amy and several other members of Atlantic

Golf Club in Bridgehampton, New York, several years ago, we went out to play six holes, and asked the players to pick a different feel state to use for their Play Boxes on each hole. "We played the first hole hitting every ball with our feet together, on the fairway and on the putting green, to access balance," Amy recalls. "It really flipped me out. At first, I noticed my own resistance. *C'mon. What's this really going to do?* Then I thought, *Wait a minute.* That was when I realized that in all my years of golf, I'd probably never played a full hole with complete commitment to each shot. On the second hole, we focused on tension. By the time you stepped up to the ball, you had to be completely committed to it. I noticed how much of the time I wasn't committed, how much of the time I actually rushed my Think Box or just wasn't fully committing or present to the shot. It made me say, *Stop, Amy. Slow down. You're here. Now do this with 100-percent commitment.*

"After we played six holes, I noticed that I was physically feeling different. I felt more athletic. This may sound strange, but I really felt like I was in a different part of my brain. I was more in tune. It was exciting. When you think about creating the conditions to help you play your best golf, I love the idea of playing this different game, one in which you're asking: *Did I really commit? Was I clear? Did I stay with the feeling until the end of my swing?* It challenges you to more deeply explore your game, to become more aware of your body, your mind, and your emotions as you play. And it's fun. I realize that most of the golf I've played in my life is mind-less. This is mind-full."

Another aspect of the Think Box to understand is how to use external and internal data. Most golfers are taught to focus on external data when they learn the game: target, wind, trees, and hazards. They aren't taught to develop their inner awareness, which can be incredibly powerful. Lynn was once at a course where she watched a legally blind golfer practice chipping from the fringe onto a putting green. The man hadn't been blind from birth, but had lost most of his sight in an accident. Before his shot, a friend helped him walk from his ball to the hole. Lynn watched him as he carefully explored the slope and the break of the green with his feet. Then he went back to his ball and chipped it. The ball went in the hole. Amazed, Lynn approached him and asked, "How did you do that? You can't see the target." And he said, "I may not be able to see it with my eyes, but I've taken in the information, and it's imprinted very strongly in my mind and my body."

Lynn thought *Aha! Our human skills offer us additional ways of gathering information about the golf course—and ourselves—if we just allow it to happen.*

Remember the little song that Bernie the Zen Master described to Jeff Bridges in *The Dude and the Zen Master*? "Row, row, row, your boat, gently down the stream . . ." Clear intent, commitment, and the ability to move into a sensory state allow us to tap into the river of intelligent energy that flows through our bodies. Prepare, become aware, and allow the process to happen.

Years ago, when Pia was working with her friend Kjell Enhager in Sweden, Kjell asked if she would participate in an experiment. Kjell had studied martial arts, and could break a piece of wood with a karate chop of his hand. He asked Pia to try this in front of a group of Sweden's national team players. Kjell said if she hesitated or deflected her *intention and attention* away from her goal before she completed the strike, she wouldn't succeed. She'd just end up bruising her hand. He told

Pia to focus on a point *beyond the piece of wood*, and direct and release all her energy to that point. She did, and the wood broke into two pieces with almost no discernible effort. The same principle applies to the golf swing. Your energy needs to be fully committed, not to the ball or to impact, but to your finish of the swing and your target.

Not surprisingly, Condoleezza proved to be a quick study. She immediately understood the concepts of Think Box and Play Box. "I've learned how to become clear and be present," she says. "I know how to transport myself from the Think Box to the Play Box now. No matter what's happening on the course, I know it's my own private space to perform."

YOUR PERFORMANCE ROUTINE: THINK BOX

GOLFERS COME FROM all over the world to attend our VISION54 programs. Whether they are mid-handicap players or professionals, we can honestly say that very few have a complete and integrated performance routine: clear decision-making, setting intention and committing to it, feeling congruency in the brain and the gut, bridging to the Play Box, and maintaining the sensory state to the finish of the swing.

The following questions and explorations are intended to help you develop a clear performance routine. Rather than asking you to think more, we want to reduce your process. If you make four practice swings before a shot, you will now prepare with one.

Think about these questions, and do these explorations on the course. And remember, once you feel your decision in your gut, go with it!

THINK BOX: QUESTIONS

- What information is important in making your shot decisions? (Checking the lie? Wind? Yardage to the middle of the green?) Simplify your decision-making. What things can you delete from your Think Box?

- When you've made a decision—let's say a 7-iron to the right side of the green—what will you do to clarify your Play Box sense or feel?

- How do you know if your gut is saying yes?

- If you make a practice swing, what's the purpose?

- Is your commitment stronger when you declare a decision out loud or feel it inside?

- How strong or confident is your voice and body language as you make your decision?

- As you prepare to step into your Play Box, what's your best way to bridge from "thinking" to "being"?

THINK BOX: ON-COURSE EXPLORATIONS

PLAY NINE HOLES and use one of these explorations on each hole.

1. On one hole, use only your instinct and gut brain; look at the target, estimate the distance, and make your shot choice. Don't gather facts or make practice swings.

2. On one hole, use extra-strong and confident body language as you make your decision in your Think Box.

3. On one hole, close your eyes, and feel yourself committing to your decision before stepping into the Play Box.

4. On one hole, use your strongest or most confident voice to state your decision out loud before stepping into your Play Box.

5. On one hole, create high adrenaline while standing in your Think Box by doing some high knee lifts, running in place, or doing jumping jacks.

6. On one hole, take two long exhales in your Think Box to lower your adrenaline before you step into your Play Box.

7. On one hole, create a happy feeling in your heart about your shot.

8. On one hole, ask yourself in your Think Box, "Do I trust my decision?" Make sure the answer is YES before proceeding.

9. On one hole, close your eyes. See, feel, and hear yourself doing what you want to do in the Play Box before stepping into your shot.

PIA: NEURO-LINGUISTIC PROGRAMMING

DURING MY YEARS on the LPGA Tour, I had begun reading about a psychological system called Neuro-Linguistic Programming. It's a methodology that helps people understand and change their behavior patterns—a set of tools for human development. *Neuro* refers to the human nervous system, including the brain and the five senses; *linguistic* refers to the verbal and nonverbal languages we use to communicate; and *programming* is the ability to manage our neurological and linguistic systems to achieve our desired results.

When I got back to Sweden, my friend and fellow coach, Charlotte Montgomery, and I traveled to Norway to take a course with an NLP-trained couple, Jorunn Sjøbakken and Truls Fleiner. They had learned NLP directly from John Grinder, one of the two Californians who created the method in the early 70s. Grinder, who was a professor of linguistics at the University of California–Santa Cruz, met a mathematician and psychology student named Richard Bandler. Both were interested in human behavior, and together began studying techniques to help people overcome their personal challenges. The two men were inspired by the work of three people: an innovative family therapist named Virginia Satir, a psychiatrist and medical hypnotist named Milton Erickson, and gestalt therapist Fritz Perls. Grinder and Bandler developed a unique system they called

Neuro-Linguistic Programming (NLP). The principles of NLP allowed participants to "describe behavior in a detailed way to allow them to make deep and lasting changes quickly and easily."

Jorunn and Truls had adapted NLP concepts into their own methodology, which they called "the discipline of communicology." Charlotte and I started using some NLP ideas with our team. Modalities are what NLP calls the five senses with which we take in information about the world: visual (what we see), auditory (what we hear—sounds and words), kinesthetic (our tactile and movement senses), olfactory (what we smell), and gustatory (what we taste). Submodalities are pieces of information we tell ourselves. NLP has an expression: *The map is not the territory.* The territory is the actual world—that is, real data. The map is our internal representation of that data, which varies from person to person. An NLP belief is that people have experiences in life, and encode the information in their brains one of two ways, negatively or positively. This applies to everything, from personal relationships to golf shots. NLP teaches people how to take a negative experience and recode it in a more useful objective or positive way. You can imagine how the wheels in my brain began spinning about how we could "recode" what happens on the golf course.

Several of the VISION54 ideas and skills we teach are based on NLP concepts. Take association and dissociation. With any event in your life, you can choose to either associate or dissociate. When you associate with an experience, you internalize and relive the feelings and emotions, which is fantastic when the experience and feelings are positive, but not so much when they're negative. When you dissociate from an experience, you observe yourself as separate from that moment, almost like you're looking down on yourself from above, or watching the experience on a screen from a third-person perspective. Your feelings become about *the situation*, not about you, and the event becomes an objective, not a subjective, feeling. Association and dissociation are powerful ways to control your emotional states. Dissociating from a bad round, or a terrible shot, is useful to playing golf. Associating with good shots and good rounds is useful to playing golf.

We taught our players (in Swedish) to "assa" (associate) or "dissa" (dissociate) on the golf course. Now that we've learned even more about how the brain stores memories, we've used these ideas to develop the Memory Box portion of the performance routine in VISION54.

When Lynn and I met in the early 1990s, we began talking about ideas that had influenced us. Amazingly, Lynn mentioned NLP. Chuck Hogan had been a fan, and she'd learned about it from him. The NLP concept that everyone brings his or her own presuppositions to an experience was huge for us. Before people work together, we believe they need to understand what their beliefs are, and how those beliefs influence us. Even though we develop a unique internal map of the world, NLP teaches that we can create new territories and behaviors based on our intentions and chosen beliefs.

As coaches, Lynn and I use NLP techniques to give feedback to players about their play. We use facts rather than subjective assumptions, opinions, or labeling. For instance, we'll tell a player, "Your swing tempo got faster on your drive on the 18th tee," rather than "You looked really nervous on the 18th tee." Instead of feeling criticized, the player is able to process that data, and recognize that their swing tempo speeds up under stress. Gradually, he or she will be able to self-manage this tendency. The methodology helps golfers become their best coaches because they learn to develop objective views of the positive parts of their game (which we call MY54) and the negatives parts of their game (NOT54).

Before we work with a player, Lynn and I make sure that we each understand our intentions and belief systems. Our intentions are to help golfers play better *on* the golf course and *enjoy* the game more. We also intend to make the art of playing golf come alive through VISION54 skills. We explicitly tell our students our beliefs at the start of each program: Bring possibility to life (=54); every person is unique; be your own best coach; and nurture positive human development and performance. That's our map of the world.

There are some who dismiss NLP as "unscientific." To that point, Lynn once read a research paper that posited that it was scientifically impossible to catch a fly ball. We're both believers in science, and we also know that, at times, science is only a partial truth.

There's true, truer, and truest. We've tried NLP. We know it works.

CHAPTER 6

AFTER THE SHOT:
MEMORY BOX

O N A SUNDAY in the spring of 2005, we were out watching the LPGA Safeway International at Superstition Mountain, not far from where we lived in Phoenix. Legendary Mexican golfer Lorena Ochoa had just birdied the 15th hole, and now led the tournament, and Annika Sorenstam, whom she was paired with, by four strokes. With just three holes to play, it looked like Lorena had the tournament in the bag as they moved to the 16th hole. Lorena had double-bogeyed the hole the day before, and shockingly, she double-bogeyed it again. Annika made her par. Now Lorena was just two strokes ahead.

They teed off on 17, a par 3. Annika made another par. Lorena three-putted from seven feet for another bogey. Now Lorena led by only one shot as they headed to the final hole. No. 18 on the Prospector Course is a par-5 hole with a long, narrow lake hugging the left side of the fairway. It's the only water on the course. Both players' drives landed in the fairway. Then Annika hit a second shot that she later described as one of the best approach shots of her career. The ball landed 22 feet from the hole. Lorena reached the green in regulation. Annika two-putted with a tap-in birdie to tie, and force a playoff.

Here's where things got really interesting. Lorena and Annika went back to the 18th tee for the sudden-death playoff. As Lorena was deciding on her shot, we watched her make the sign of the cross in the equivalent of her Think Box. Then she stepped into her Play Box. She had a 3-wood in her hand. Shockingly, she drop-kicked her shot; the club took a divot on its way to the ball, and she yanked it left into the water. Victory to Annika.

Because Arizona is close to Lorena's home in Mexico, she had a group of about 200 people—close family, extended family, friends, and fans—following her that day. When she finally walked off the 18th green, they all gathered around her, crying and hugging her, trying to console her. It was like a funeral. We looked at each other and didn't even need to say the words aloud: *Lorena needs to be extremely careful about how she stores this memory.*

Another of the essential lessons to understand about golf is the importance of memory and how it affects performance. It's why we have made Memory Box the dramatic finale to the Think Box–Play Box performance routine.

Memory is powerful. It's a central construct of our identities. Memory is the physio-neural mechanism by which we encode, store, and recall information important to our lives. Memory gives us the capability to access previous experiences, as well as to adapt to new ones. Neuroscientists describe memory as the retention, reactivation, and reconstruction of an experience-related internal representation. In other words, when we experience something, it gets imprinted and internally represented in specific areas of our brain, particularly the amygdala, which is in the oldest part of our brain.

Long ago, memory literally helped us survive. We needed to identify and remember dangerous things that might kill us—snakes or lions, for instance. Memory enabled us to avoid them and survive. The same mechanism still works in our brains today. For instance, as children not knowing better, we might touch a hot stove and burn our hand. We experience the sensory and emotional feeling of pain, and we might cry. Our brains store the association—hot stove = pain—as a memory. The more emotionally charged the event or experience, the stronger that memory will be. Here's the fascinating thing: Our brains don't make a distinction between a snake and a hot stove, or a hot stove and a golf hole that gives us fear. They're all the same to the brain, if it associates the object with danger.

Several months after Lorena's disaster in Phoenix, we were at the U.S. Women's Open at Cherry Hills Country Club in Denver. In the final round, Lorena was three strokes behind the leaders at the turn, and making a thrilling Sunday charge. With four birdies on the back nine, she had taken the lead by one stroke as she approached the 18th hole. The 18th hole at Cherry Hills is a par 4 with water hugging the left side. It was similar enough to the 18th hole at Superstition Mountain in Phoenix. Lorena and her caddie had an intense conversation before she took the tee. She was holding a 3-wood in her hands. She looked tentative. As she swung the club, she came out of her shot and drop-kicked the club into the dirt—just as she had done in Phoenix. The ball veered left into the water. Lorena finished the hole with a quadruple-bogey 8 to lose the tournament by four strokes.

Johnny Miller, who was commentating for NBC, quickly connected the two events. "Lorena did the same thing earlier this year in Phoenix," he said with astonishment. He then showed a side-by-side comparison of her two swings. "This seems to be a pattern," he said, identifying the error as a repeating technical flaw in her swing.

A couple of months later, we ran into a friend of Lorena's. "You need to hear the rest of the story," the person told us.

Our source shared that as Lorena stood on the 18th tee at Cherry Hills, she said to her caddie, "I'm not sure about this. I feel like hitting a 4-iron." Her caddie argued with her. "You're playing great, Lorena," he said. "There's plenty of room for you to hit a 3-wood on this hole."

"But I feel like hitting the 4-iron," Lorena insisted. Her gut was telling her to hit a different club. And she let her caddie talk her out of it.

Johnny Miller had identified her problem as a repeating technical glitch in her swing. He was right about the technical glitch, but only partly. Miller was going with external cues. The other truth, in our opinion, was an internal cause: Lorena's stored emotional memory showed up in her technique.

Let's analyze what happened to Lorena at Cherry Hills through the filter of memory. She approaches the 18th tee and sees the hole with water on the left. It's the last hole of the tournament, the pressure is on, and she has a 3-wood in her hand. Her brain recognizes it as similar to the hole at Superstition Mountain. Lorena's brain sends a signal: *Water on the left! Hot stove! Snake! Danger!* It was telling her to do something—*anything*—different, so she wouldn't repeat the result. Lorena tried to ignore her gut instinct to hit her 4-iron. But if you've touched a hot stove, the brain will always remember it.

Here's another super-important fact about memory. Psychological research has shown that humans have a 3:1 negativity bias as our default setting in storing memories. The brain naturally stores negative memories faster and stronger than positive ones. Neuroscience and evolution give us a simple explanation. It was much more important to remember danger and threats long ago than to remember positive or happy incidents. If we remember the snake and the hot stove, we are more likely to avoid them—and survive. On the other hand, when we store negative memories, consciously or subconsciously, we are prone to triggering those memories and emotions when we encounter similar experiences.

Recently, we conducted an informal experiment. We asked golfers in the middle of a round, and after the round, how things were going. Nearly everyone said something negative. "If I hadn't missed that shot on the 14 hole, I'd have had a great round."

"Those three-putts really killed me." We describe our own games more negatively than those who are watching us, which is why we need to be aware.

We need human skills to neutralize negative memories, and store positive memories more strongly. If Lorena had been prepared to address this situation properly, she might've finished off that U.S. Open win.

Here are the simple facts of golf. When we're ready to hit, the ball is sitting at Point A. We use a club to propel it to Point B. Point B could be the middle of the fairway, in the water, off the property, and sometimes, Point B could even be in the hole. Point is, there is always Point B.

Then there's you, the golfer—an emotionally complex human who is extremely invested in Point B, that is, the outcome of the shot. When we hit a good shot, we feel exhilaration: *Wow! My ball's on the green six inches from the hole!* We celebrate, we high-five our partners. But because it's not good etiquette to celebrate too much, we quiet down and move on to our next shot.

When we hit a shot that lands in the water, disappears into the deep rough, or soars out of bounds, we curse ourselves, slam our clubs, or find something to blame. *Damn, it's in the water! I hate this hole! I let my elbow fly out again!* Depending if your past experience was positive or negative, when you face a similar shot in the future, you'll find yourself feeling relaxed and confident, or you'll walk up to the ball and think, *Uh-oh.* Your body might begin to feel a little tension. Absolutely nothing has happened yet, but your palms are getting sweaty. Unfortunately, the memory function in the brain doesn't have a delete button. It doesn't move our bad shots to the trash.

Remember, the brain stores negative memories three times more strongly than it stores positive memories.

So what can we do?

The Memory Box is the third and final part of your performance routine. Using the Memory Box skill, you can learn to be emotionally objective and neutral after bad shots, and reinforce your positive emotions after your decent, good, or great shots. For us, there are two things that are useful to evaluate after every shot: your process (how you executed your Think Box and Play Box) and your outcome (the quality of the shot and where the ball landed).

Let's review. You've decided on your intended shot in your Think Box, and committed to the sensory feel to use in your Play Box. Here's your first Memory Box practice goal: After you hit a shot—any shot—hold your swing until the ball comes to a stop. The 15 to 20 seconds after your swing are vital to how your brain stores a memory. By pausing and staying in your Play Box, or even taking a few breaths as you put the club in your bag, you'll avert a premature negative emotional response to the outcome of the shot. When the ball lands, allow yourself only two reactions: objective or positive. Make these the only two choices for your Memory Box, if you want to fulfill your potential as a golfer. We're not telling you to forget your bad shots—we're asking you to be objective about them.

You may categorize your Think Boxes and Play Boxes as Not Good, Good Enough, Good, or Great. Your reaction to your shots and processes that are Not Good will be objective; your reaction to Good Enough, Good, and Great shots and processes will be some degree of positive feeling. An objective reaction states the facts: *The ball is in the bunker; I lost my balance in the backswing.* You will store Good Enough, Good, and Great shots and processes with a positive feeling. Being positive to your Good Enough shots is one of the secrets to optimal performance. It's not about lowering your standards, but about seeing and playing the game with the right mind-set. Move on, and look at the trees, sing a song, or count the dimples on your golf ball as you head to your next shot. We guarantee you will play better, and enjoy yourself more.

Alternatively, soak up the experience of your Good Enough, Good, and Great shots. And absolutely celebrate, internally or externally, your Good and Great shots. In doing this, Memory Box becomes the all-important third step of your performance routine.

Here's how Memory Box might look in different situations on the course. In Scenario 1: You stroke an important putt for birdie, but the ball slides three feet to the right of the hole. You say to yourself, "Okay, I obviously misread the break, so next putt, I'll pay closer attention to reading the green (I'm being objective). But I'm happy about how I stroked the ball and held my motion to the finish. I kept my Play Box focus on finishing my stroke, so I'm positive and happy about my process and the stroke—good."

See? No negative memories.

Scenario 2: You pull your drive into a bunker. Again, your reaction is to stay neutral and objective to the outcome: "Okay, the ball is in the bunker, but I'm confident about my bunker play." What about your process? You wanted to swing at 70-percent tempo in your Play Box, but instead you swung at about 110 percent of your normal tempo. Next time, you'll deepen your focus on your tempo and try to be more present in your Play Box. You're neutral and objective about your swing, which is your process. You're not denying what happened, but you're not beating yourself up, either. Your Memory Box for this shot is neutral to outcome, neutral to process. You won't store any negative memories.

Scenario 3: You're a scratch golfer and you hit a wedge from a great lie to 20 feet left of the flag. You know you didn't stay with the feeling of "soft shoulders" all the way to the finish. You chose to be objective to your process, but you're still putting for birdie, so the outcome is Good Enough.

Or, you hit a fade off the tee. You wanted to hit a draw, but it ends up a lot shorter than you anticipated. You're objective to your process, since you didn't stay with your Play Box long enough, but you're in the fairway and have a good chance to hit it on the green. So the outcome is Good Enough.

Scenario 4 (this is extreme, but that's why we like it): You mis-hit your tee shot on a par 3, and the ball never gets airborne. It keeps rolling, but somehow the ball ends up in the hole. We'd be totally yippy-skippy about the outcome—a hole in one!—and we'd stay neutral and objective about the process, which was hitting it thin, and our center of gravity got really high. In this scenario, we're positive to outcome and neutral to process. No negative memories.

The important human skill is exercising choice about your

reaction to your shots. Manage your reactions. Don't be blasé about your good shots. Give yourself a pat on the back, or a good fist pump, and *feel* some degree of happy. We see players who hit great shots and act like it's a routine event, because they're overachievers and think they should be hitting great shots all the time. But they're hurting themselves by not storing positive memories. This skill isn't about the power of positive thinking. It's about the necessity of understanding your brain's negativity bias and creating neutral or positive emotional states after your shots. Your brain will take care of the rest.

If we had been Lorena Ochoa's coaches, this is how we might have worked with her after her debacle: First, we would have told her, "Listen to your gut's 'no' signals." If your gut is signaling it doesn't like the shot or the club, step out of the Play Box. Change your club, choice of shot, or Play Box focus. Make sure you have a "go-to" shot you can use under extreme pressure. Understand that these situations will happen, and be ready to shift your plan of attack. If you see water on the left and your gut brain reacts, trust it. Hit your 4-iron, or a fade with your driver, or hit a low punch shot with the 3-wood. First and foremost, listen to yourself. Do not step into the Play Box if you're trying to force something. Instead, make a change.

We work continuously with players on Memory Box skills, so they'll learn to be factual and objective to bad shots. And we work on creating more positive memories to store. Sometimes players will need to re-create the situation of a negative memory to override it. Lorena could have gone back to the 18th hole later that evening, or early the next morning, and created some Good Enough, Good, and Great memories to store. She also could have worked on re-creating those situations in visualization or imagery on the range. She could have become neutral about the original shot, then stored a positive memory about her process.

All players need to train these Memory Box skills. Pia has trained her own skills for so long, they've become habit. She's Positive Pia.

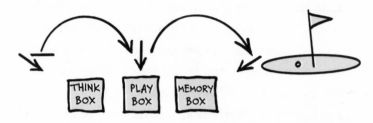

We've seen extraordinary turnarounds in people's games with this one skill. Suzann Pettersen took control of her Memory Box, and learned to be more objective about her missed shots and more positive about her good ones. Interestingly, youngsters who take our junior clinics get this right away. One 12-year-old boy started nodding when we explained Memory Box and blurted out, "Oh my gosh! I wish I had learned this when I was 8." The other thing kids regularly say to us is, "Could you please teach this to my parents?"

One more point: Positive and negative memory storage can endure long after the shot. For amateurs, when you're having a beer at the 19th hole after your round, be aware of what you and your friends are talking about.

"Did you see my shot that went in the water?"

"I can't believe how many three-putts I had today."

"If I hadn't hit that shot into the rough on 16, I'd have had my best score of the season."

Professional golfers need to take extra care of their Memory Boxes. If they triple-bogey or three-putt a hole during a tournament, reporters will surely ask them about it afterward, likely over and over again. The players need to be mindful about how they answer. Annika Sorenstam became a master at this skill. If she was asked about a double bogey she'd made, she would answer, "Yes I double-bogeyed that hole, but it was what happened afterward that was important. I committed to every swing after that hole, and I came back." She refused to over-emotionalize a mistake and replay it.

PGA Tour pro Chris DiMarco learned the skill after he finished playing a round with Tiger Woods at the Masters. DiMarco was listening while Tiger did his interviews. Tiger talked about how well he hit the ball during the round and the great shots he'd made. Afterward, DiMarco shook his head. "I just played with the guy. He hit it terrible out there today!" At that moment, he says he realized that Tiger was taking control of his memories of the round. Tiger had an important skill he didn't have. DiMarco began to practice it, and it led to big changes in his career.

"I've observed that if most professionals have one weakness, it's their Memory Boxes," says former PGA Tour player and VISION54 student Arron Oberholser. "Good players tend to be proficient with their Think Boxes and Play Boxes, because that's the heart of playing at a high level. If you're a player who's breaking 70 on a regular basis, you've probably got good skill-sets in your Think Box and Play Box. But when you're competing under intense pressure, and you're not able to put aside a poor shot, that's what separates the winners from the rest of the field." Arron added: "For my career, taking control of Memory Box was the thing that elevated my game to the next level."

Russell Knox knows that Memory Box skills can make a huge difference in performance. "You can have two equally talented golfers standing next to each other hitting the ball identically, and one of them goes out and wins the tournament, and the other one goes out and misses the cut," Knox says. "You're like, 'Okay, what's the difference between those two?' One of them reacts negatively to his poor shots, and allows his emotions to get control of him. He has no chance against the player who can control his emotions, and his outlook, during a round. Far too many people, professionals and amateurs, spend a lot of time complaining. You hit a shot that's not quite what you wanted it to be. You get down on yourself. But golf isn't a game of perfection. It's about managing your bad shots and your emotions. Most times, those shots will be good enough." When he hits a so-so shot, Russell says he catches himself on the verge of complaining, and he hears Pia's voice. *Is it good enough? You're still going to be able to make a par. It might not be a birdie, but it's good enough.*

Russell used his Memory Box skills to near-perfection when he won the WGC-HSBC Champions in Shanghai in 2015. When he made the turn on Sunday, he was tied for the lead with Kevin Kisner. Russell birdied holes 10 and 11 to give himself a two-shot advantage.

"I was thinking to myself, 'Okay, I trust my short game, and I trust my recovery game. Don't get mad at yourself if you hit it in a fairway bunker, hit it in the rough, or miss a green. Trust your ability to make a par.' That day I hit some shots that weren't great, but I didn't store them in a negative way. They were good enough. I kept making pars, and eventually I birdied 16, which gave me a three-shot lead with two holes to play.

"It's something I'm going to keep with me for the rest of my life," Russell says. "Golf is a tough game. When you're out there under pressure, you have to be good to yourself and not beat yourself up. Being so close to winning, I knew I couldn't afford to be negative. I remember thinking that even if I hit it in the water on one hole, I'm going to stay objective to the outcome and tell myself, 'That was a good swing, Russell.' "

PERFORMANCE ROUTINE: MEMORY BOX

ON THE COURSE, we don't use the word *practice* very much, because we tend to think about it differently than most people in golf. Some golf clubs have explicit policies in their rule books: NO PRACTICING ON THE COURSE. Their interpretation of practice is hitting lots of extra balls, taking extra chips around the green, and putting several putts—which beats up the course and holds up play. That's why we prefer to say we're going out to "learn," "train," or "explore" on the course. Look at these questions and explorations as a new kind of practice.

Memory Box skills don't come alive until you put them in context on the course. This is where our patterns and negativity biases show up, something that doesn't happen on the range. Do these Memory Box questions and explorations. Keep practicing them!

WHAT WAS?
○ GREAT
○ GOOD
○ GOOD ENOUGH

MEMORY BOX: QUESTIONS

- What do you normally say to yourself after a good shot? What do you feel? How about after a bad shot?

- How well can you close the door on the past, and move on to the next shot with all your attention?

- When you play, can you reflect on your commitment to the process before focusing on the outcome of your shot?

- What is your best strategy to be objective, neutral, and factual after a shot you didn't like?

- What is a "Good Enough" shot for you?

- How strongly do you store or emotionalize your Not Good, Good, Good Enough, and Great shots and processes?

MEMORY BOX: ON-COURSE EXPLORATIONS

PLAY NINE HOLES, and practice one of these explorations on each hole:

1. On one hole, distract yourself for 10 seconds before choosing how you respond to each shot.

2. On one hole, say something objective or factual about each shot you've hit.

3. On one hole, first evaluate if you've committed to your selected shot and Play Box. After that, evaluate the outcome of the shot by being objective or happy.

4. On one hole, say something nice about each process you engage in or each shot you hit. Be authentic.

5. On one hole, don't make any commentary after your shots. Feel happy or objective.

6. On one hole, keep your body language strong, and your chin high, after each shot.

7. On one hole, feel and store a positive emotion for an extra 10 seconds after each shot, or Play Box that was Good Enough, Good, or Great.

8. On one hole, after any shot that is Good, Good Enough, or Great, take a long and deep breath.

9. On one hole, feel your heart "beam" in response to any shot that is Good, Good Enough, or Great.

DURING THE ROUND

BETWEEN SHOTS—
YOUR BODY, MIND, AND EMOTIONS

AS WE'VE POINTED OUT, golf is a sport in which players spend relatively little time swinging the club, compared to how long they spend on the course. During a four-hour round, a golfer will spend 30 to 45 minutes actually hitting a shot, and at least three hours in between shots. What you do with your body, mind, and emotions between shots can either help or hurt your chance of creating a good performance state for each shot.

The part of golf that is not technical often gets lumped into a broad phrase called "the mental game." Bobby Jones once quipped, "Golf is a game that is played on a five-inch course—the distance between your ears." As Tom Watson said, "The person I fear most in the last two rounds is myself." And Johnny Miller observed, paraphrasing Thomas Edison, "Golf is 90 percent inspiration and 10 percent perspiration."

We don't believe it makes sense to think about golf as simply physical or mental. Golf is physical *and* mental—plus technical, emotional, social, spiritual, and more. Each of us can experience one of these aspects as less or more important at different times. Take Lynn, for example. She finds her golf challenges today are more physical than mental, since her main obstacle is being less flexible than she used to be. And yet, all the parts of the game remain integrated.

The 30 to 45 minutes while you're hitting your shots will

always be most important because that's when you're actually *playing* golf. The time spent in your Think Box, Play Box, and Memory Box is at the core of your game. However, what you do during the three to four hours *between* shots will greatly influence your performance. We hope to help create a paradigm shift, so you can use your human skills—managing your body, your mind, and your emotions—to positively influence your ability to swing the club and strike the ball.

There's a growing body of work about how humans achieve mastery in disciplines as varied as medicine, chess, music, and sports. Dr. K. Anders Ericsson is a professor of psychology at Florida State University who specializes in the psychological nature of expertise and human performance. He and two colleagues came up with the concept that "deliberate practice" leads to mastery in many domains. (Malcolm Gladwell popularized this theory and the so-called 10,000-hour rule in his book *Outliers: The Story of Success*.) But according to Ericsson, it isn't just the number of practice hours; a person must constantly push beyond his or her comfort zone, honestly identifying weaknesses and using feedback and new strategies to achieve improvement. Condoleezza Rice talks about how she practices a new piece of piano music. "It's not just learning the notes," she says. "If you look at my score, you'll see that I write down all kinds of instructions to myself. I even write down where I should breathe."

In short, players need to practice much more than technique. They need to learn to master all of their human skills on the golf course.

We've read many of the classic management (and self-management) books over the years, from Stephen Covey's

The Seven Habits of Highly Effective People, to Jim Loehr and Tony Schwartz's *The Power of Full Engagement*, to Daniel Goleman's *Focus: The Hidden Driver to Excellence*. Many of the authors deal with how people can stay engaged at work, minimize workplace errors, and avoid burning out. Loehr is a psychologist and co-founder of the Johnson & Johnson Human Performance Institute, and Schwartz is a former journalist and founder of an enterprise called the Energy Project that works with organizations, coaches, and individuals to create workplaces that are healthier, happier, and higher-performing. In *The Power of Full Engagement*, Loehr and Schwartz write, "Every one of our thoughts, emotions, and behaviors has an energy consequence, for better or worse. The ultimate measure of our lives is not how much time we spend on the planet, but rather how much energy we invest in the time we have."

Their premise is that performance (as well as health and happiness) is grounded in the skillful management of energy. Each of our four human states—physical, mental, emotional, and spiritual—produces and consumes energy. Managing them is essential to success, in whatever field you choose.

During the 1980s and 1990s, psychologists began to study something called "flow." The work, pioneered by American psychologist Mihaly Csikszentmihalyi, deals with the mental state in which you're fully immersed in performing an activity, feeling energized focus, complete involvement, and enjoyment. He called it flow because the people who had experienced it compared the feeling to being carried along by a current of water. During flow, human emotions are positive, energized, and aligned with the task at hand. The person has a deep focus on the activity. Another psychologist, Roy Palmer, proposed that flow, or the "zone," might also influence move-ment patterns, because better integration of the conscious and subconscious reflexes improves coordination. Many athletes describe a feeling of near-effortlessness during performances when they achieved their personal bests.

Another social scientist we've become intrigued with is Amy Cuddy of Harvard University, who studies body language and its relationship to success and power. Nearly 35 million peo-ple have watched Cuddy's 2012 TED Talk, "Your Body Shapes Who You Are." Her work shows that something as simple as body language can change feelings of power, behaviors, per-formances, and outcomes.

Our view is that we need to acquire a wider understanding of ourselves—and our capabilities to become the best pianists, artists, surgeons, and golfers that we can be. How do we man-age our bodies, minds, and emotions to help create flow states and discover peak performance? We believe that human skills give us the entry point and the tools. As the saying goes, "We are the ones we've been waiting for."

WHAT CAN YOU DO BETWEEN SHOTS
TO MANAGE YOUR BODY, MIND, EMOTIONS?

CHAPTER 7

YOUR BODY:
WALK TALL, CREATE POSITIVITY

A T LONG LAST, golfers are beginning to get smarter about the importance of our physical health. We know it's important to warm up our muscles before we play. We know it's important to hydrate and eat on the course. But for many players, this still just means hitting a few balls on the range before teeing off and stopping at the halfway house for a hot dog and a beer.

In 2012, we attended a seminar in Phoenix organized by Nike Golf and led by Gary Gray, a physical therapist who has pioneered an area of study called Applied Functional Science. Gary runs the Gray Institute in Adrian, Michigan, just south of Ann Arbor, and teaches biomechanics—the *why, how,* and *what* we move when we perform a task, whether it's kicking a soccer ball, shooting a basketball, or swinging a golf club. This includes everything from the work of our muscles, joints, tendons, and proprioceptors to how gravity, mobility, and stability affect movement.

Gary said that one thing that perplexes him about golfers is that many don't seem to see golf as a sport. "They hit a shot, hang out, hit a shot, sit in a cart, hit a shot, eat something, hit a shot, and hang out some more," he says. He stressed that golfers need to do more during the round (when we are not hitting the ball) to keep our bodies awake, particularly to the three planes of motion—forward and back, right to left, and rotational—that

define a golf swing. "Why don't golfers do more between shots
to make themselves more athletic?" he asked. "Why don't they
run around, do jumping jacks, stretch their hips, or take extra
breaths—things we know will deliver immediate results?"

Gary is one of many smart people in golf performance today.
We're also great fans of Dr. Greg Rose and Dave Phillips of the
Titleist Performance Institute (TPI), as well as their advisory
teams. They point out a simple fact—many golfers aren't flexible
enough or strong enough to get into the positions their instructors are asking them to in order to swing the club properly.

In terms of the biomechanics of the body, there's something
called the "Joint by Joint Approach"—a term first coined by
Gray Cook, a physical therapist, and Mike Boyle, one of the top
strength coaches in the world. They describe the human body
as a "kinematic chain," in which joints relate to one another.
Cook teaches that the athletic body works in an alternating
pattern of stable parts connected by mobile parts, and if this
pattern is broken, negative results occur. Our friend Greg Rose
explains it this way: "Our feet need to be stable when hitting a
golf ball. Ankles, the next joint up the chain, are mobile, and
move with our bodies. The knees should remain stable, while
the hips create mobility and coil in the golf swing. If our bodies
are in sync, this kinematic chain operates perfectly. But if this
pattern of movement is disrupted, the entire chain of motion
can be compromised. For example, if a player loses mobility in
his or her ankles, the feet may respond by becoming unstable.
This is a common compensation as the body seeks mobility
somewhere, which then throws off the entire kinematic chain.
The knees then go unstable, causing excessive motion in the
lower limbs, and the hips respond by limiting mobility. If your

hips are now not moving or loading properly, you're not going to be able to hit the golf ball very far."

Golfers can and should be aware of whether their body's kinematic chain is working properly. But to Gary's point that golf is a sport and golfers are athletes, we need to understand that sitting in carts or standing and waiting to hit shots causes our hips and ankles to get tight, and so the feeling in our proprioceptors and limbs can actually turn off.

Remember, proprioceptors are the body's internal GPS system, the network of sensory receptors in our muscles and joints that allow us to detect basic motions and positional changes. There are simple ways to keep your proprioceptors engaged. Greg Rose says walking, hitting balls, or training barefoot are the simplest ways to train your proprioceptive system. As we've mentioned, taking off your shoes increases movement in the foot and ankle, and helps stimulate the proprioceptors. We have several students who hit balls a couple times a week on the practice range barefoot or in socks. Others will take their shoes off for a minute or two before they tee off. We coached an LPGA Tour player who is 5-foot-2. We saw her gain 10 yards with a 5-iron just by practicing hitting with her shoes off. She used her feet properly, and her kinetic chain responded.

Golf involves long periods of inaction, punctuated by short bursts of intense energy when we swing the club. We often hear players saying, "I started the round horribly, but then I played great." Or, "I was loose on the practice tee, but I played the first few holes like an idiot." The main thing to understand is that your body doesn't remain static before and during a round. It's always changing. When you start swinging poorly, it's often because the state of your body has changed.

Golfers need to stay athletic as they stand, walk, or wait between shots. How the body turns off or tightens up will be different for everyone. If your hips lock up, a good exercise is to take a few steps forward and back with your feet pigeon-toed, then a few steps forward and back with your toes pointed out in a duck walk. If your glutes turn off, do a few squats to turn them back on. If your shoulders tense up, loosen them by rolling them forward and back, or try doing "progressive relaxation," which is to tighten a muscle group and then slowly relax it.

What we put into our bodies before and during a round makes a huge difference in regulating our body's energy levels. Our colleague David Leadbetter was one of the first golf coaches to be interested in nutrition. Pia remembers meeting David during her early years on the LPGA Tour, and his bookshelves were already filled with tomes about nutrition and performance.

David explains that patterns of shot-making are often linked to the highs and lows in energy patterns that occur during four to five hours on the course. "Say your worst scoring average tends to be on holes 12, 13, and 14," he says. "It could be that your aerobic capacity isn't what it should be (and that you need more aerobic training), or that your energy level tends to drop at this point in the round, and you may need to eat and drink more to boost your energy. It's all about your specific patterns; if you become aware of those patterns, you can change them for the better."

Today it's rare to find elite players who don't carry water, electrolyte-fortified sports drinks, nutrition bars, and nuts in their bags. They understand the importance of blood-sugar levels, and how allowing them to get too high or too low can affect their play.

Another way the body affects performance is through our adrenaline levels. Adrenaline, also known as epinephrine, is a hormone created in the adrenal glands, which sit above our kidneys. Adrenaline is one of the chemical messengers in our sympathetic nervous systems. When we perceive a threat, adrenaline jolts our "fight or flight" responses, sending blood surging to our hearts, lungs, and brains. Our blood pressure rises, our hearts beat faster, and in extreme situations, people can lift exceptionally heavy objects, or literally run for their lives.

An important skill in golf is the ability to manage our adrenaline levels and heart rates while we're playing. When we get into stressful situations—think of the tee shot at the island-green 17th hole at the Players Championship—not only will you feel your heart pounding, you might hit your ball 20 yards over the green with that extra adrenaline. By recognizing that your adrenaline level will spike under stress, you can bring it down before your shot by taking several long, deep breaths or doubling the length of your exhale to your inhale. This calms your autonomic nervous system and quickly lowers your adrenaline level. (You may still need to grip down on your club or hit a shorter one if you're leading a tournament!)

Conversely, if you're feeling sluggish or tired from heat, or you're enduring a long, slow round, you can increase your adrenaline level by doing a few jumping jacks, running in place, or taking a series of long, sharp inhales and shorter exhales. This is what powerlifters do just before they lift huge weights in order to increase their adrenaline.

Understanding the tendencies of your adrenaline levels is key. Some players hit better shots when they have higher adrenaline. Some players hit better shots with lower adrenaline. Tour players who perform better with high adrenaline include Tiger Woods, Sergio Garcia, Suzann Pettersen, and Keegan Bradley. Pros who perform better with low adrenaline include Jason Day, Inbee Park, Lydia Ko, and Ernie Els (whose nickname is "The Big Easy"). The point about adrenaline levels is that great golf can be played both ways. That's why it's important that each golfer knows his or her optimal adrenaline state. Again, as variable human beings, and as players, different situations will create (and require) different adrenaline levels. We need to know which situations require dialing it up or down.

Alonzo "Lonnie" Knowles and Teri Hjelte are husband-and-wife golf coaches based in Wilmington, North Carolina. They're competitive players who are avid students of performance. Lonnie and Teri came to us several years ago for a one-day coaching session. We didn't have a lot of time, so we went straight to the golf course to observe them in real-time playing situations. We asked them what other sports they did. Lonnie and Teri are free divers, which means they dive vertically without scuba gear, regulating their breath and heart rates to reach impressive depths. We thought about how their free diving might relate to their golf. What we learned was amazing.

Lonnie explained that free divers use a technique called "breathe-ups" before a dive. They concentrate on totally relaxing with long, slow breaths for up to 20 minutes, which lowers the heart rate by 10 to 50 percent, increases blood oxygen, and rids the body of carbon dioxide. We suggested to Teri and Lonnie they play nine holes creating different situations in which they accelerated their heart rates (by jogging in place or hyperventilating), then slowed down their heart rates (by taking long, deep breaths or with visualization). In one situation, a challenging approach shot to a green, Lonnie slowed down his adrenaline and heart rate with deep breathing. "My focus improved immediately," he says. "My state of mind when I swung the club was much clearer. Overall, when I concentrated on doing this, my shots were better and more consistent."

He also discovered that when his adrenaline level increased, and his heart was racing, "I couldn't perform at all. Now I understand that when I feel myself getting nervous or excited, I need to lower my adrenaline and slow myself down."

Teri, on the other hand, found she performed better when she raised her adrenaline level and heart rate. "There are times when my energy gets too low," she says. "I used to think that was just me, that I tended to be calm and focused. But when I increased my energy level, I saw much better results in my shots."

It was fascinating to see how two bodies performed best with such different adrenaline and heart-rate states. Once Teri and Lonnie knew their optimal states for different situations, they could use their human skills to regulate their bodies. We believe that if golfers and their instructors worked for five minutes during each lesson exploring different performance states, they would see dramatic results.

Another human skill important for performance is body language. Most people might think body language is just a matter of good or bad posture, but increasingly, golfers are beginning to understand its significance. In 2015, Jordan Spieth missed the cut in the first two FedEx Cup playoff events. Afterward, he said, "I promise you when I travel to Chicago for the third event, my body language will be very, very different."

What did Jordan mean? And why is body language important?

Let's turn to a woman who has done some fascinating work in this field. Amy Cuddy is a social scientist at Harvard University who studies the effects of body language on performance and success. Her central proposition is that by assuming a physical "expansive" pose associated with power—standing tall and taking up physical space with your arms outstretched—you can actually make yourself feel more confident, whether it's before an important job interview, a presentation, or a performance. Your body posture and movements communicate directly with your brain chemicals and hormones, specifically DHEA and cortisol, creating feelings of positivity and confidence or negativity and stress. As Cuddy puts it, "Our bodies can change our minds, our minds can change our behavior, and our behavior can change outcomes."

"Research shows that in pressure-filled situations, when we are distracted by thinking about possible outcomes of our performance, our skills are measurably diminished," Cuddy writes in her book *Presence: Bringing Your Boldest Self to Your Biggest Challenges*. "When we explicitly monitor ourselves, second by second, any task that requires memory and focused attention will suffer. We don't have enough intellectual bandwith to perform at our best and simultaneously critique our performance. Instead we're caught in a faulty circuit of trying to anticipate, read, interpret, and reinterpret how other people are judging us, all of which prevents us from noticing and interpreting what's actually happening in the situation."

Remember how human beings store the memory of negative experiences three times more strongly than positive ones? What if we could manage our bodies to create a positive physiological bias?

Cuddy, who studies hormonal responses to social stimuli, has investigated how the core muscles we use to hold expansive, or "power," poses can influence our emotions, and thus our DHEA and cortisol levels. Any time we have an emotion, hormones are released in our body. The main adrenal hormone released when we have positive emotions is DHEA, also called the "youth" or anti-aging hormone. (Synthetic DHEA is illegal to use in athletic competition because it has been proven to enhance performance.) When we experience negative emotions, the primary hormone released is cortisol, otherwise known as the stress or aging hormone. Cuddy's research indicates that a slouching posture can trigger the release of cortisol, which slows down the body's reaction time and clouds decision-making. On the other hand, she says, confident body language can trigger the release of DHEA, which improves performance.

As part of our VISION54 programs, we now ask students to play a few holes with a strong posture, energetic stride, and an elevated gaze. We ask them to confidently voice aloud their intention for a shot: "I'm going to hit a low draw around the bunker to a back left pin."

We've seen this work. Yani Tseng is a talented LPGA Tour player who had won five majors by the time she was 24, and was ranked No. 1 in the world for 109 consecutive weeks from 2011 to 2013. In 2010, we were at the Women's British Open at Royal Birkdale. Yani asked to speak to us. "I've lost my confidence," she said. "I don't know what to do."

We took a blank sheet of paper from one of our blue VISION54 notebooks and said, "Yani, we know you've played a few really good rounds this summer. Tell us what you did well." Her caddie was with her, so together they wrote down a few things.

She was able to conclude: "I'm doubting myself in my Play Box. And I'm having lots of negative thoughts when I'm on the course—I'm sure the other players can tell just by looking at me that I've lost my confidence."

We helped Yani develop some simple things she could do that week to raise her confidence and improve her performance. One of those things was stronger body language—to walk taller, manage her self-talk, and sing to herself between shots to initiate a sensory state and keep her mind from defaulting to negative thoughts.

We traveled back to Sweden, where we watched the rest of the British Open on television. We saw Yani walking down the fairways with her head up, her shoulders back, and a big smile on her face. She didn't hit the ball perfectly during the final two rounds, but she won the tournament.

Another of our students, J.C. Anderson, the teaching pro in St. Louis, also tried the body-language technique. "I was at a VISION54 program in 2012," he says. "We went out to play three or four holes while Lynn and Pia observed us. They said something that seemed like a passing comment at the time. " 'J.C., we notice that when you're on the course, you're looking down at the ground most of the time. Why don't you try keeping your chin and head up between shots. Look up at the horizon, or above the tree line, when you're walking and when you step onto the tee.'

"It sounds like a funny little thing," J.C. says, "but this one tip pretty much changed my golf game and my life. Not only do I literally see more on the golf course, I'm seeing things more positively. We've all heard the expressions 'Keep your head up' or 'Keep your chin up.' They're metaphors. They're telling us to dig deeper for that positive attitude toward life. Keeping my head up opened my chest; standing tall improved my posture and my breathing. My game improved dramatically. In fact, this might have been the best golf advice I've ever gotten."

As with adrenaline and body language, tension is relatively easy to monitor on the course. Even walking down a fairway, try doing a body scan between shots. Are you holding tension in your shoulders, your jaw, or your neck? Focus on relaxing those areas.

We're in awe of scientists doing this kind of work. Amy Cuddy and her fellow pioneers might not realize it, but in addition to helping people prepare for job interviews and presentations, they've done a great service for the world's golfers.

DURING THE ROUND: THE BODY

ONCE GOLFERS TEE OFF, many become passive on the course. They're waiting for a good shot to happen, or to feel better rhythm, or for the momentum of their games to turn around. We've heard players say, "I just don't have it today," which is a pretty broad statement for an athlete to make.

In our view, being proactive about your physical state on the golf course is one of the easiest, and most important, of your human skills.

You're responsible for yourself. You need hydration and fuel to keep your energy levels up for four or five or six hours. You need to keep your joints and muscles loose, and maintain good balance and movement, to swing the club well. Along with awareness and management of adrenaline, these relatively simple things will determine the success of every drive, fairway shot, pitch, chip, and putt.

THE BODY: QUESTIONS

- Before you tee off, do you check how your body is feeling? How often do you need to check in during the round? How flexible do you feel?

- Do you notice your adrenaline level? Is it generally high or low, and how does that relate to how you're playing? Can you increase your adrenaline? Can you lower it?

- What are you eating and drinking between shots and holes? Are you keeping track of how you're playing at different points in your round? Do your scores rise if your energy falls?

- What's your body language on the course? How does it make you feel?

- Do you have any common tension spots in your body? How do they affect your swing? How can you manage tension between shots?

THE BODY: ON-COURSE EXPLORATIONS

EXPLORE ONE OF THESE EXERCISES on nine different holes during a recreational or practice round:

1. Play one hole doing a body tension scan between shots. Where do you feel tension or tightness? Where do you feel loose? Start with your feet, and go all the way up to your neck and jaw.

2. Play one hole with a low adrenaline level in your Think Box. Before each shot, take two long exhales. Walk slowly and calmly. This will lower your adrenaline.

3. Play one hole with high adrenaline in your Think Box.

Before each shot, do a few jumping jacks or jump up and down. Do you swing better with high adrenaline?

4. Play one hole pretending that the pace of play on the course is fast. Walk faster and with more energy between shots to raise your adrenaline level. Use shorter routines before your shot. Create a great Play Box.

5. Play one hole pretending that the pace of play is slow. Walk deliberately between shots. Stand very still before it's your turn to hit and create your best possible Think Box and Play Box.

6. Play one hole; between each shot, squat and take 10 "duck steps" (with your toes pointing out) forward and then 10 "pigeon steps" (with your toes pointing in) back. These exercises keep your quadriceps and hips active.

7. On one hole, make two left-handed practice swings (if you're a right-handed golfer) before each shot. If you're a left-handed golfer, make two practice swings with just your right hand.

8. On one hole, walk between shots with weak body language, slumping your shoulders and with your eyes on the ground.

9. On one hole, walk between shots with tall and strong body language. Keep your eyes on the top of the tree line or the horizon.

What did you learn from these explorations? What helps you get in a more athletic physical state while playing?

PIA: JOANNE WHITAKER—

THE DOCTOR IS IN

DURING THE MID-1980s when I was playing on the LPGA Tour, I reached a point where I knew I needed something besides continually working on my swing to improve my game. My friends and fellow pros Kelly Fuiks and Charlotte Montgomery suggested I look up a woman they knew named Dr. JoAnne Whitaker.

JoAnne was a pediatrician and a psychiatrist who was also an exceptional golfer. She'd played since she was a young girl, and had won the Florida Women's Amateur Championship several times while she was in college. David Leadbetter (who is now married to Kelly) and Chuck Hogan would send players to JoAnne who needed non-technical help (that is, everything else!).

I drove up to see JoAnne at her home near Tampa, Florida. She told me about herself, and how she had completed fellowships in hematology, oncology, and nutrition. (She would later develop one of the first and most accurate tests for Lyme disease.) She had also spent a great deal of time in Asia, helping start a medical school and nutrition lab in Thailand, and developing research and training programs for Vietnamese physicians at the Children's Hospital of Saigon. During the course of her experiences in Southeast Asia, JoAnne became deeply interested in Eastern philosophy, with its emphasis on the relationship between the mind and body.

The first thing JoAnne asked me to do when I met her was to take the Myers-Briggs personality test. Afterward she told me, "Pia, I think if you take this again in a couple of years, it's going to come out very differently. I have a feeling you're going to become *more of who you are,* not who you think you're supposed to be."

She was absolutely right. I'd always been the good girl who did what I thought others wanted me to do. I had tried to please my family, my teachers, and pretty much everyone in my life. JoAnne was the first person to urge me to focus on defining myself.

JoAnne also introduced me to meditation—which she called "learning to focus." She lit a candle in her living room and said to me, "Pia, can you sit with this candle for five minutes and just look at the flame and the colors without thinking about anything?" I'd never tried it before, and I gave it my best effort. I started to see things I'd never seen in a flame: shapes, movements, and the smoke rising. The candle practice was one of the ways JoAnne taught players to focus on visual images for a long period of time, in order to access the sensory parts of their brains.

Along with Chuck Hogan, JoAnne was one of the first people in golf to think about "balance," in terms of utilizing both sides of the brain to play good golf. I'm pretty sure she was the first person who told me to "let go" of technical thoughts when I stepped up to the ball, and to move my awareness to where I wanted the ball to go.

I still have one of JoAnne's worksheets from 1984. On a piece of paper, she had sketched the two lobes of the brain with a line connecting them. She titled the left lobe "left/conscious," and inside the lobe she wrote the words *logical, analytical, parts,* and *verbal.* Inside the other lobe, which she titled "right/subconscious," she wrote the words *intuitive, synthesis,* and *wholes.* Above the line connecting the two lobes, she typed the instruction "Cross Over." (JoAnne also used the words "ROBOT" and "GOSSAMER" to describe the left and right brains, proving she was as much a poet as a scientist.)

During her career, JoAnne authored many scientific studies. One was called "Breaking Records in Golf by Balancing the Autonomic Nervous System." Her report looked at numerous holistic/alternative therapies, including meditation, Feldenkrais, Rolfing, reflexology, Reiki, and Healing Touch/Quigong, among others. She wrote, "Our brain must exercise whole brain thinking, using the right and left sides of the brain. If we think only with our right brain, and try to visualize the shot we want to hit, we will usually goof because the yardage is wrong, and the club selection is wrong. On the other hand, if we play golf using only the left analytic brain, we will make the proper club selection and have the yardage correct, but because we are unable to visualize, the process that communicates to the body exactly how to execute the shot will fail, and the result is a poor shot!" She went on, "Today, to break records in golf, it takes more than just being in the zone. Our whole body, mind, and spirit must be like a precise instrument."

JoAnne was a "waker-upper." She encouraged me to listen to myself, to be courageous, and to broaden my perspectives— to learn and grow. I wasn't looking for the meaning of life when I met JoAnne—I was simply looking for practical ways to become a better golfer. She helped me understand the difference between *thinking about* being an athlete and *being* an athlete. JoAnne was "out there" in the best sense of the term. She was ahead of her time.

CHAPTER 8

YOUR MIND:
MANAGE YOUR SELF-TALK

WHEN PIA STARTED TO WORK with the Swedish national teams, she wanted to pay more attention to what was going on in the minds of her golfers while they were on the course. At the time, she was working mostly with the younger players, but the women from the senior team approached her and asked her about giving them some coaching help, too. Pia remembers them as well-behaved, upper-class ladies who loved golf but didn't have a lot of confidence. So she and Charlotte Montgomery embarked on an experiment. They asked the group, "Please say aloud all the things you say to yourself before, after, and in between your shots on one hole, and remember what you said. Then tell the rest of us."

One woman announced, "Before a shot, I've said to myself, *Don't mis-hit this drive like you did yesterday.*" Another lady reported, "I've said to myself, *I can't believe that shot went into the bunker. You're a total loser.*" Charlotte and I were shocked, as one lady after another admitted talking to themselves, and judging themselves, in extremely negative ways. "I'd never speak to another human being the way I speak to myself," one of the women said later. She had no awareness of her internal monologue while she was playing. It was a revelation.

We call our internal conversations "self-talk." Other people call it the monkey brain, which is an endless cycle of random thoughts that lead us in a million directions. Neuroscience research says we have upward of 70,000 thoughts a day. Where do all these thoughts come from? Are they accurate? Does anyone fact-check them? Or are they the work of some sabotage-minded monkey sitting on our shoulder?

In reaction-based, shorter competitions, athletes don't need to spend as much energy or skill managing their internal conversations. The 100-meter sprint world record is 9.58 seconds—not much time for negative conversation in your brain. A professional sumo match can take as little as three seconds.

Other sports, however, are endurance contests that can challenge the mind as much as, if not more than, the body. In 2010, American tennis player John Isner took 11 hours and 5 minutes (over three days) to beat Frenchman Nicolas Mahut at Wimbledon. They played 183 games, the longest match in tennis history.

The longest playoff in golf history took place in 1949. Cary Middlecoff and Lloyd Mangrum both shot closing 69s in regulation during the final round of the Motor City Open. Middlecoff, who had just won the U.S. Open, and Mangrum began the sudden-death playoff tied after nine holes, matching each other with eight pars and a birdie. As darkness fell, they met with tournament officials and decided to play two more holes, halving both with pars. At that point, they were declared co-champions.

Even in a normal round of golf that takes three, four, or five hours, the mind can become a decisive factor in performance. It can help elevate us to the height of performance—or drag us down. We became interested in what kind of internal conversation or "self-talk" helps performance, and what kind hurts performance. Our purpose was to develop a human skill that would help golfers manage their self-talk.

In 2009, we were invited to Morocco to speak to the International Society of Sport Psychology. While we were there, we interviewed several psychologists who had done research on athletes and self-talk. One of them, Judy van Raalte of Springfield College, said self-talk was a huge factor in how athletes performed, and showed us how thoughts create feelings, feelings create behaviors, and how those behaviors then reinforce our thoughts. That's how we gained a better understanding of the dangerous self-talk feedback loop.

Here's how it works. You hit a bad shot, and you say to yourself, "I'm an idiot." Then you start to feel like an idiot. And then you start behaving like an idiot, getting angry or slamming your club. By that point, you *have become* an idiot. It's no different from saying, "I'm a crappy putter." After you miss the putt, it tends to become a fact. Then you continue to putt badly. We call this looping. It's also a self-fulfilling prophecy.

Golfers have three choices: Quiet the mind, let the thought float away (meaning, don't give it any attention), or distract and manage it.

Some meditative techniques help the mind open and discard its thoughts. Other techniques can help focus. Then there's the kind of meditation practiced by some Buddhist monks, who center their attention on positive emotions such as love and kindness. We meditate every day, so we find it fun and interesting to explore different styles and how they apply to golf.

For golfers in general, we find targeted sensory focus to be the most practical way to abort the self-talk feedback loop. For instance, Lynn's brain often loops into the past, so she likes to quiet her mind by getting more physical—feeling her feet and wiggling her toes in her shoes. Our minds go to where we put our attention. Doing mini-meditations, or "being present" drills, on the course for 15 to 20 seconds helps to break a self-talk loop, and raise present awareness through your senses. If you're headed toward negative self-talk, look at the trees, listen to the birds, or feel the breeze on your neck while your partner is hitting.

We also love the exercise of playing a hole in complete silence—with no talking, either to your playing partners or inside your own head. For some, this becomes a very peaceful and restful experience. Others find it impossible. (As we say, you get good at what you practice, and you don't get good at what you don't practice.) Many golfers spend too much time engaged in self-talk during a round.

Self-talk becomes destructive when it focuses too much on the future or the past, especially if we obsess about things out of our control. But can self-talk be useful if it's aligned with our goals and who we want to be? To test that idea, we asked students to write down how they wanted to talk to themselves between shots. When they went on the course, we asked them to replace any unproductive self-talk with more productive self-talk (which you believe—anyone can say positive things, but "I'm a great putter" can backfire if the person doesn't really believe it). Instead of walking up the fairway thinking, *If I miss this green, it's a sure double bogey*, they'd say to themselves, *I've hit a lot of good chips lately*, or, *This is a fantastic golf hole. I'm so good at committing to my decisions.* During the 2016 U.S. Women's Open, Brittany Lang would approach her ball on the course and say to Luke, her caddie and brother, "What a great lie I have!" The specifics of the positive self-talk aren't as important as the function it plays in crowding out negative thoughts. Pia describes it as

"good brainwashing." Was it a coincidence that Brittany won the U.S. Woman's Open?

The first time PGA Tour pro Kevin Streelman came to see us, he said, "I have a confession. When I stand over the ball, I sometimes have thoughts that I'm going to hit it out of bounds, or I'm going to pull it. Sometimes I'm standing over the ball, and I say to myself, *Kevin, you're going to hook it.* Or, *Kevin, you're going to three-putt.* Do other golfers do this?"

We said, "Well, yes, Kevin. Everybody does it. That's the human condition." He was incredibly relieved. He thought he was the only one.

One of the first things we did with Kevin was help him understand that the voice in his head didn't define him. This comes from meditation research. "It's just a thought," we told him. "It's not who you are. You don't have to believe it."

So, what is the best way to counter negative self-talk? The first step is to identify it. Notice if you're thinking too much about winning the match, or worrying that the 18th hole doesn't suit your fade. Then distract or cut off those thoughts. Start counting your steps. Sing a song. Tell a joke to your caddie. We don't care what you do, but the more quickly you catch your unproductive bias and shut it off, the better you'll perform. W don't tell players what kind of self-talk to use. It's up to you wh works best, but you need to make it congruent with who y are, and what your goals are, so that you can believe it.

Pia was once with a group of male teaching pros at Mu field in Scotland. The course doesn't have par during reg play—the sign just tells the player how many yards the ho "I was playing from the back tees, so I knew it was long," Pia, "but I didn't know if it was a long par-4 or a par-5 l

just played it as best I could, but I had a totally different at tude. I wasn't saying to myself, *If I don't reach the green in two, I won't make par.* Or, *This is a short par 5, so I should make a birdie.* I would have automatically started creating unproductive expectations in my mind. But I didn't, because I didn't know. I was like, *Wow, this is different.*"

Research indicates that when it comes time to perform, no self-talk is best. Learn to quiet your mind and be completely present through your senses in the four to nine seconds of your Play Box. When you're on the golf course and you start thinking about things that aren't helpful—*Am I going to lower my handicap today? I pulled those last two shots*—cut the loop by counting your steps or talking to someone. Don't let self-talk take over your brain.

We like to tell our students the story about Annika Sorenstam, when she won the U.S. Open in 1995 at Pine Needles in North Carolina, and again in 2006 in Newport, Rhode Island. At Pine Needles, she was about to tee off on Sunday, and her brain was going berserk with self-talk: *Am I going to be able to keep my lead? What if I don't keep my lead?* She decided before the round what she would say to herself before and after every shot: *Fairway, green. Fairway, green.* It was an intentional mantra she used to calm her monkey brain.

Kevin Streelman played in 152 PGA Tour events before he won his first tournament. He was playing in the Tampa Bay Championship in 2013, and after the second round, he knew he was performing well enough to beat the field. Before the third round, he knew he would have to control his self-talk to achieve his goal. He told his caddie that if and when doubt crept into his mind, they would sing songs and recite Bible verses. And that's

what they did. In quieting his unproductive self-talk, Kevin went bogey-free over the last 37 holes. He didn't miss a shot on the last 11 holes of the final round, and he shot a 4-under 67 for a two-shot win over Boo Weekley. If you ask him how he broke through on the PGA Tour, he'll tell you, "I stopped my negative self-talk."

BETWEEN HOLES:
THE MIND AND THE POWER OF SELF-TALK

WHEN WE SPEND TIME working out in the gym, we get stronger. But which muscles are we strengthening? Are they the correct ones for what we want to accomplish? Are there additional muscles we should be strengthening that we're ignoring? The mind is one of the foundational "muscles" for golf, and strengthening your mind will be very, very useful for your game.

BETWEEN HOLES: THE MIND: QUESTIONS

- What do you say to yourself between shots?
- Does your mind tend to be focused, scattered, monkey brain, critical, or positive?
- On the course, do you focus on things under your control or things that aren't under your control?
- Does your mind often go to the future, the past, or to outcomes such as your score or where your ball landed?
- Do you focus on what is going well on the course?
- Do you expect perfection?
- Do you give your mind a break between shots?

• What do you say to yourself when you play well? How does that differ from what you say to yourself when you don't play well?

THE MIND: ON-COURSE EXPLORATIONS

DO ONE OF THESE EXPLORATIONS on each hole for nine holes:

1. Put five tees in your right pocket. Any time you notice unproductive or negative self-talk, move one tee to your left pocket. How many tees do you have remaining in your right pocket at the end of the hole?

2. Play one hole, and notice any unwanted self-talk. Once you're aware of it, distract yourself with a song, counting, or talking to your playing partners.

3. On one hole, observe your surroundings in between shots without describing them in words.

4. On one hole, when you notice your self-talk, say it out loud or write it down.

5. On one hole, say something positive about yourself between each shot.

6. On one hole, imagine your best friend talking to you while you play.

7. On one hole, alternate listening to the sounds around you without describing them between shots, and scanning your body to notice how it feels.

8. On one hole, write down three self-talk sentences you like, and read the sentences to yourself between shots.

9. On one hole, play with no self-talk whatsoever. Can you
   be fully present and aware to what you see, hear, and feel
   without describing it, reflecting on it, or talking about it in
   any way? It could be the beauty of nature, the sensation of
   your feet striking the ground, or the sounds of birds and
   the wind around you.

CHAPTER 9

YOUR EMOTIONS:
RESILIENCE AND CATCHING YOURSELF MID-SCREWUP

RUSSELL KNOX SAYS he hears Pia's voice in his head when he's competing in a tournament. "When I hit a so-so shot and I'm just about to complain or make a stupid comment to myself, Pia is always there," he says with a laugh. "She's saying, 'Is your shot *good enough*, Russell? I'm sure it is. You're still going to be able to make par. It might not be the best shot you've ever hit, but it's going to be good enough. You'll be okay.'"

Every player encounters setbacks on the golf course. This is the nature of variability. You will misjudge or mis-hit a shot. The weather will take a turn for the worse before your tee time. Your ball will hit a sprinkler head. Then, there are times when bona fide disaster strikes, usually in the greatest pressure moments: Greg Norman's collapse at the finish of the 1996 Masters; Lorena Ochoa drop-kicking her drive into the water on the 18th hole at the 2005 U.S. Women's Open; Ariya Jutanugarn's implosion during the last three holes of the 2016 ANA Inspiration; Jordan Spieth's quadruple-bogey 7 on the 12th hole of the 2016 Masters; or Phil Mickelson's disastrous 18th hole at the 2006 U.S. Open.

Now we're going to tell you a disaster story about one of the players we coach. This should illustrate both the challenge and the power of using your human skills in the most stressful situations you'll encounter.

Russell Knox has lived in Jacksonville, Florida, for almost 15 years. He has played TPC Sawgrass's Stadium Course more times than he can remember. During all those years, he has never hit a tee shot into the water at the par-3 17th hole.

During the third round of the 2016 Players Championship, Russell stepped onto the tee box of the famous island-green 17th hole and prepared to hit. He was 8 under par, among the top-10 players in the tournament. Russell lined up his pitching wedge for the 122-yard shot. It soared into the air, and came down inches short of the right side of the green, gently splashing into the water. Russell looked stunned. His shoulders slumped.

Instead of heading to the drop zone, he re-teed his ball. As soon as he hit, his body language showed he had shanked his second shot into the water, too. He shook his head, and hit his club on the ground in frustration. Then he teed the ball up for a third time. He hit again. This time he blocked the shot slightly to the right. The ball splashed into the water, close to where his first ball had entered. Dropping his club, he grabbed his head in disbelief.

Johnny Miller was commentating on television. "I feel for him," he said with genuine anguish. "This is a fishbowl, and Russell's under the microscope right now."

This time, Russell and his caddie walked to the drop zone. He hit his seventh shot safely across the water, and onto the green. Walking to the island green, he tipped his cap to the crowd. Then he two-putted for a 9, tying for the fourth-highest score recorded on the hole in tournament history. Russell finished his third round with an 80.

"It was an epic fail," he admitted afterward to a reporter.

"I thought I hit a good first shot. I thought I'd stuffed it. It's such an easy shot when you have no nerves or adrenaline in play. But it's a different story once you've hit two in a row in the water. The green feels like the size of a quarter. After that, everything goes so quickly. Your blood is just pumping through your brain. Until you're in that position, you don't understand what it feels like."

We were really proud of Russell. After the hole, he understood precisely what had happened to him. He practiced textbook emotional resilience later that day, and came back on Sunday to shoot an amazing 67 to finish in a tie for 19th place. Before his round on Sunday morning, he tweeted to his 11,000 followers, *SHANK you very much for all the nice messages. Looking forward to getting my revenge today!!!* A few days later, he tweeted again, putting his performance on No. 17 in context: *Golf has given me my career and SO much more. Let's keep growing the game and opening people's eyes to our sport.*

EMOTIONS. WHERE TO BEGIN? According to relatively new research at the Institute of Neuroscience and Psychology at the University of Glasgow, we humans have four fundamental emotions. Three are so-called negative emotions: fear, anger, and sadness. The fourth, and only positive, emotion is happiness.

When a golfer misses consecutive shots, the experience creates strong negative emotions: shock, panic, and anxiety. Your body begins to release hormones that have a direct effect on how you perform. Cortisol is the body's "stress" hormone. It's composed of the same base molecules as the "happy" hormone, DHEA, and the two hormones work on a fulcrum, constantly offsetting each other. When we have high levels of DHEA, we have low levels of cortisol. When we have high levels of cortisol, we have low levels of DHEA.

As we mentioned earlier, DHEA is a performance-enhancing hormone that, among other things, acts as a lubricant to the brain. When your brain receives information while your body is experiencing higher levels of DHEA, you have access to your highest brain and motor functions. It's as if the brain and body are a smooth-running engine. This enables your best decision-making, visual acuity, balance, timing, and rhythm. While higher levels of DHEA don't guarantee greatness, they do guarantee *access* to your fullest potential.

On the flip side, when cortisol spikes in your system—as it did in Russell's—the brain basically says "Access Denied." Instead of sending information and instructions seamlessly through your brain and body, the engine begins to stall. Decision-making suffers—or it shuts down completely. You literally don't see as well, and your balance, timing, and rhythm lose their coordination. Russell's brain essentially froze as his cortisol soared. After hitting his first ball into the water, he teed the ball up for a second and a third time. Spectators must have been asking, *What is he thinking?* And that's precisely the point. He wasn't thinking.

This is why it's important to understand what's happening physiologically when you mis-hit a shot under pressure. If you do, you'll be able to use your human skills to recover.

In explaining the concept to our students, we like to use this illustration of the adrenaline-DHEA-cortisol grid.

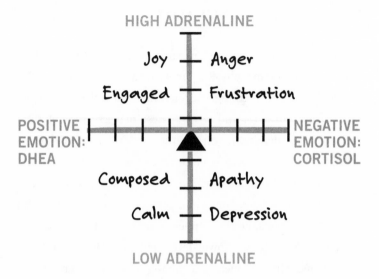

HIGH ADRENALINE

Joy — Anger

Engaged — Frustration

POSITIVE
EMOTION:
DHEA

NEGATIVE
EMOTION:
CORTISOL

Composed — Apathy

Calm — Depression

LOW ADRENALINE

Hormones and emotions influence one another. They also interact with your adrenaline level. As you look at the grid, the vertical line is your adrenaline level. The horizontal line is your DHEA-to-cortisol continuum. In the upper-left quadrant, you have DHEA and high adrenaline. These golfers are having one of their best days on the course; they're happy and engaged, with great access to all their mental, physical, and emotional skills. Words associated with DHEA and high adrenaline are *joy, passion, pride, exhilaration, happiness, engagement, courage,* and *inspiration.* These players are having a party on the outside (if they're extroverts) or on the inside (if they're introverts). Some players who show DHEA, high-adrenaline behavior (when they're playing well) include Jordan Spieth, Tiger Woods, Suzann Pettersen, and Michelle Wie. (It's an interesting exercise to observe the pros, and watch where they are in their quadrants.)

Now let's move to the upper-right quadrant: high adrenaline and cortisol. Players in this quadrant are having a terrible day on the course, or have just made a huge error.

Adrenaline and cortisol are surging, shutting down their access to their best physical, mental, and emotional skills. Words associated with high adrenaline and cortisol are *anger, frustration, anxiety,* and *terror.* These players are exploding or imploding, depending on whether they're extroverts or introverts. Extroverts throw clubs, curse, and kick their bags, and introverts fume silently. Players associated with cortisol, high-adrenaline behavior (when playing badly) include John Daly, Tiger Woods, Dottie Pepper, and Suzann Pettersen.

Next let's go to the lower-left quadrant: DHEA and low adrenaline. These players are having a peaceful day on the course, with great access to all their skills. Words associated with DHEA and low adrenaline include *calm, composure, fulfillment, ease, contentment, compassion,* and *appreciation.* Players who exhibit DHEA and low-adrenaline behavior include Jason Day, Dustin Johnson, Catriona Matthew, Inbee Park, and Annika Sorenstam. (Oh, and you can probably add the Dalai Lama to this quadrant.)

The final quadrant is cortisol with low adrenaline. These players probably started out the round poorly, and are discouraged and demotivated. They have poor access to their abilities, and have pretty much given up on their round. Words associated with cortisol and low adrenaline include *apathy, depression, self-pity, withdrawal, burnout, resentment, guilt,* and *boredom.* Players who are in the cortisol, low-adrenaline quadrant (when not playing well) include David Duval, Ernie Els, Sergio Garcia, and Na Yeon Choi, as well as many professionals going through a tough time or becoming tired of tour life.

One amusing story we have concerning these quadrants is about one of the owners of the Chicago Bears football team who came to our VISION54 program. He listened to us talk about DHEA and cortisol, and said, "I want my running backs, my receivers, and my quarterback in high DHEA. I want my linemen in high cortisol." One of our coaches, Kristine Reese, said to him, "I don't think so. High cortisol is when you're going to get your penalties."

Of course, not all players are squarely in each quadrant. Most players are somewhere in the middle, so their behaviors are less extreme than the ones we've described. The important thing is understanding the adrenaline-DHEA-cortisol grid and how to develop your human skills to manage what's happening. We see tour players arriving at the course in higher-cortisol states if they've gotten stuck in traffic or overslept. We also see cortisol rising during warm-ups if they don't feel they are hitting the ball the way they want, and they'll start getting anxious and down on themselves. You might be on one side of the grid during a round, until you put a shot into the water. The challenge is how quickly you can recognize your reaction and do something to get back to the other side. We call it "bounce-back" ability, or emotional resilience. One little shot of cortisol is like a paper cut; it's not going to overwhelm you. But if it gets bigger, you're going to start hemorrhaging. If Russell Knox had quickly recognized his reaction to his first shot going into the water at the 17th hole at the 2016 Players Championship, he could have stepped away and regrouped. He could have chosen a different club, ball flight, or Play Box, or played his next shot from the drop area. Because he didn't, he hemorrhaged.

Human skills allow you to counter cortisol buildup by understanding that you need to elevate your DHEA. You can also focus on increasing your reservoirs of DHEA, so you stay on the good side of the grid. But the best way to raise your DHEA when you need to is by creating positive emotions. Remember, these are *feelings*, rather than *thoughts*, and they will be unique to each person.

The University of California–Berkeley's Greater Good Science Center, which studies the psychology, sociology, and neuroscience of well-being, has published studies indicating that highly effective ways of raising DHEA include summoning feelings of gratitude, humor, or appreciating your natural surroundings. In less stressful situations than disaster during a final tournament round, former PGA Tour player Arron Oberholser raised his DHEA by *becoming present* to the natural beauty around him on the golf course—the trees, flowers, and mountains. During a tournament round, 2016 U.S. Women's Open champion Brittany Lang makes a point to think about things she's grateful for, such as her husband and her dog. (This is essentially why we carry around photos of our friends and family in our wallets. They invoke feelings of love and gratitude.)

Building DHEA is building emotional resilience. Building emotional resilience is a human skill. It's putting another club in your bag. You're creating a protective force field. Negative things happen on the golf course. When they do, how do you recognize what's happening, and how can you limit cortisol and increase DHEA? Even better, how do you preemptively build emotional resilience?

For Russell, an emotional-resilience strategy on the 17th hole might have looked like this: He would have been aware that his cortisol and adrenaline would spike after hitting a shot into the water. He would have understood he needed to lower them, so he could have taken several deep breaths to bring down his adrenaline, and he could have recalled the hundreds of good shots he'd hit on that hole to create positive feelings. He would have chosen a Play Box sensory feel, and the shot easiest to execute at that moment (that is, his best, deepest Play Box feel, and a conservative and dependable "go-to" shot). He might have made sure to hit with 70-percent tempo all the way to the finish of his swing, knowing his adrenaline was sky high. And he would have aimed for the widest part of the green.

Pia likes to use herself as an example to illustrate diagnosis and strategy. "I play my best when I have lower-to-medium adrenaline and some DHEA," she says. "On the way to the course, I listen to music I love in order to build my DHEA. Before warming up, I meditate for a few minutes to access calmness. During my warm-up, I can tend to go into the future and begin to worry, so often I'll take long, deep breaths to lower my adrenaline (and commit to a few things under my control). I'll hit shots with slow tempo. I also do my best to stay away from complainers. Then I'm ready."

There's an excellent awareness exercise you can practice on the course to keep track of your emotional states. Draw the adrenaline-DHEA-cortisol grid in your yardage book or on your scorecard. Put an X where you play your best golf. Are you playing well when the X is higher or lower on the adrenaline axis? Where do you play your best on the emotional axis? Is it in the upper-left quadrant when your adrenaline and DHEA are high?

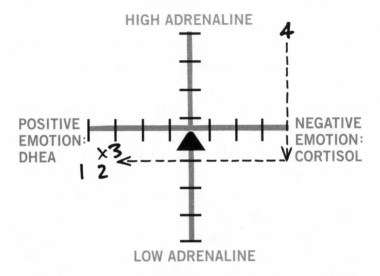

HIGH ADRENALINE

POSITIVE EMOTION: DHEA

NEGATIVE EMOTION: CORTISOL

LOW ADRENALINE

Write down the number of the hole you just played on the grid. Place it where your DHEA and adrenaline levels were. In the illustration above, the player is in lower adrenaline and DHEA after the first three holes. Something happens on the fourth hole to spike the player's adrenaline and cortisol, so she or he will want to lower adrenaline and access a positive feeling before teeing off on hole 5. After the round, look at where your numbers appear on the grid.

These emotional management and resilience skills are ones you can practice continuously during a round. For instance, on the second hole, you hit a couple of great shots and end up with an eagle. Your adrenaline has risen, so what do you need to do before you tee off on the next hole? You need to take some longer exhales to lower your adrenaline. You're able to do so and par the hole, but on the next hole, play slows down, which really bugs you. You make a double bogey. What do you need to do? Access something that makes you feel happy, calm, or grateful to create more DHEA. We guarantee that if you come off the

18th green with more DHEA in your system than when you started the round, no matter what your score is, you're now in charge of your game and your body—you're resilient. If you're playing a tournament, you've got a human skill in your bag that your opponent might not.

Our VISION54 coaches, Kristine Reese and Tiffany Yager, love to tell a story about playing with some of the young male professionals who work in the Scottsdale area. "They're in their mid-20s, and they work on their swings all the time," says Kristine. "I don't spend too much time on my game right now, but we play fun matches with them. They're cortisol junkies, and we'll watch them get more and more upset if they don't like their shots. When we reach the 12th hole, we press our bet."

Returning to the idea of the explicit and the implicit, great players used to practice these implicit human skills—even if they didn't quite know what they were. Ben Hogan would drive to the course very slowly. It was his way of getting his state more regulated. Suzann Pettersen used to watch a sports event, or an inspiring movie like *Rocky*, before a later tee time. Ariya Jutanugarn listens to her favorite music before she tees off.

Think about things in life that affect our golf games. If you're late to the course and have only five minutes to warm up, the last thing you want to do is hit balls on the practice range. You're setting yourself up for an anxiety attack and spiking cortisol. If you only have a few minutes, what makes most sense? It would be much better to create positive emotions—do some balance, tempo, and tension exercises, and put yourself in a good state. That's being mindful instead of mindless.

Emotional resilience, DHEA and cortisol awareness and management, are not skills we generally learn—or can put on autopilot. They're necessarily subjective. Did I create cortisol with my negative reaction to that three-putt? What can I do to get back some DHEA before I hit my next tee shot? Some rounds will really test us, so it's important to keep building this bank of emotional resilience. If this is especially important for you, check it before going out to play, and every so often during your round. The long-lasting effect occurs when you start with a lot of DHEA in your system; that is what it is to be emotionally resilient. Don't wait until the tank is empty.

One crucial finding by researchers has been that it takes humans six to 10 hours of sleep to reestablish baseline levels of DHEA after an upsetting experience. That means if your cortisol spikes sky-high on a hole, or builds up over a few holes, it's not likely you can restore the balance right away or even during the round. Russell Knox made sure to get a good night's sleep that Saturday night, which restored his DHEA-cortisol balance. And he was able to play his final round in a positive state.

Dr. Al Petitpas is a sport psychologist whom we worked with at The First Tee for many years. He says the greatest skill an athlete can learn is to "catch themselves in mid-screwup." That's being a Master of Variability. That's emotional resilience. That's using your human skills. It's worth many strokes on the golf course.

Russell has become a true believer. Even though he wasn't able to catch himself "mid-screwup," he used emotional resilience after his blowup on No. 17 to raise his DHEA levels before he teed off on Sunday morning.

"Everyone wants to be a perfectionist," he says. "But golf isn't a game of perfection. It's about managing your bad shots and your emotions. At this point in my career, I feel like how I manage myself is way more important than my actual shots."

DURING THE ROUND: EMOTIONAL RESILIENCE

EMOTIONAL RESILIENCE is among the most important human skills you can develop—on and off the course. We want to accentuate the point that emotional resilience is a skill, not just a concept. It's a skill you can practice before a round, between shots, and between holes (and between events in your life, too!). Like many golfers, you might tend to be too outcome-dependent in general. External factors annoy you, such as a bad bounce, slow play, or bogeying a hole. Emotional resilience is important because you're on the course for many hours. Be proactive about your emotional state—not reactive. Build DHEA before you step onto the course, and keep refining it during play.

EMOTIONAL RESILIENCE: QUESTIONS

- What situations tend to "get" to you emotionally on the course? Think of several specific examples and what happened as a result.
- What adrenaline level is best for you, high or low? How can you manage it on the course?
- What can you do to create more positive emotions on the golf course?

• What can you do before a round to ensure you start off feeling emotionally resilient?

EMOTIONAL RESILIENCE: ON-COURSE EXPLORATIONS

PLAY NINE HOLES doing one of these explorations on each hole.

1. On one hole, alternate playing shots with low adrenaline, medium adrenaline, and high adrenaline. How were they different? Which worked best for you?

2. On one hole, actively access at least 15 seconds of positive emotions between each shot, and release any tension you might feel in your body.

3. On one hole, create a state of being calm, content, and composed between every shot.

4. On one hole, create a state of being excited and pumped up between every shot.

5. On one hole, make yourself feel irritated and frustrated, then see how quickly you can return to a more positive state and adrenaline level before your shot.

6. On one hole, emotionally fall in love with each shot before you hit it.

7. On one hole, skip for 20 seconds between each shot.

8. On one hole, smile between shots so others can see you; smile to yourself inwardly and feel the emotion.

9. On one hole, notice when unwanted emotions intrude, and concentrate on letting them float away.

LYNN: THE BEAT OF HEARTMATH

THE GOLFING BRAIN has always fascinated me—my own brain, and the brains of our students. At the beginning of my coaching career, I was still trying to figure out how to teach most effectively. One day I said to Chuck Hogan, "Chuck, I've been reading about the brain and how it works." Chuck interrupted me and started rattling off the theories of developmental psychologists Jean Piaget and Joseph Chilton Pearce, an American writer on human and child development, who investigated connections between the brain and the heart. Chuck talked about how the brain develops, and how we form behaviors. If any other golf pros would have been there, I'm sure they would have nervously backed out of the room and run to the lesson tee.

"Here's the secret to golf," Chuck said. "Emotionalize what you want, and dissociate from the rest." In other words, take in the positives on the golf course, and separate them from the negatives. It was the same idea about association and dissociation that Pia brought to her Swedish teams. I caught my breath and thought, *Wow, that kind of makes sense.*

I read one of Pearce's books, *The Magical Child*. It was pretty heavy, but his ideas were provocative. Interestingly, he described the anatomical heart as a "compassionate mind," an organ with control functions that rivaled those of the brain.

Flash forward to 1997. I read an article about how scientists had determined that the heart communicates with the brain via the vagus nerve. The vagus nerve is the longest cranial nerve. It contains motor and sensory fibers and, because it passes through the neck and thorax to the abdomen, has the widest distribution and effect in the body. The article broadened into the topic of stored memories, particularly those associated with traumatic events and their clinical aftermath, which is post–traumatic stress disorder (PTSD). I was impressed with the argument that we could actually affect the "wiring" between the amygdala, where our long-term memories are stored, and the heart. That led to something called "coherent heart-rate variability."

I faxed the article to Pia, who was in Stockholm. The very next day, she faxed back an article from *Svenska Dagbladet*, a major Swedish newspaper. It was an article on the very same subject she had read the day before. *This is serendipitous*, I thought.

Not long afterward, I was giving a lesson. I told my student that the latest science showed that she could choose to store the memory of a particular shot, or choose not to store it. She looked up and said, "Oh, this reminds me of HeartMath!" She explained she was referring to a research center in California called the Institute of HeartMath. I thought, *Okay, these are three serendipitous events. Let's go.*

So Pia and I traveled to the Institute of HeartMath for one of its trainings. We found ourselves in a room with psychiatrists, heart surgeons, and other doctors. They looked at us and said, "You guys are golf pros. What are you doing here? HeartMath deals with stress. Is there much stress in playing golf?"

HeartMath's training program gave us insight into brain and heart science. When you're in a happy, positive, and confident emotional state, the rhythm between your heartbeats is smooth. This means there is coherence among the brain, the heart, and the nervous system. Decision-making is quicker, and more sound. Emotional stability is easier to sustain, and physical coordination is enhanced.

When you're in a stressful state and experiencing emotions like frustration, anger, and anxiety, the rhythm and time between beats become uneven, which interferes with the communication between the heart and the brain. Blood vessels constrict and blood pressure rises, which limits the brain's ability to process information smoothly, including decision-making and problem-solving. It also negatively affects your physical performance.

We learned that negative memories get stored three times stronger than positive memories. Thinking about how this related to golf, we became convinced that the emotions we associate with our memories—whether it be annoyance, irritation, or frustration on the negative side, or calmness, happiness, pleasure, and satisfaction on the positive side—can influence our access to our best performance abilities for the rest of the round and beyond.

One day, Dr. Rollin McCraty, the HeartMath Institute's executive vice president and director of research, was explaining the concept of neuroplasticity, and how signals from the heart could rewire neural pathways and synapses in the brain and affect stored memories in the amygdala. Surrounded by these medical professionals, I raised my hand. "Is that why Ben Hogan got the yips?" I asked.

I'll never forget the look on his face. He hesitated and said, "I'm not sure."

I was sure. It made total sense to me that the yips could result from an amygdala that just keeps firing negative stored memories, causing the heart to beat erratically and the nervous system to seize up.

One message I took away was this: Under emotional pressure, people tend to revert to past negative memories and associations if they don't affirmatively decide that they want to store their current activities, emotions, and memories more positively.

At our VISION54 schools, we now teach players how to regulate their coherence levels using a HeartMath app called Inner Balance. To use it, you plug a sensor into your iPhone and insert an earpiece. A pacer on the app prompts you to moderate your breathing, which, while generating positive feelings, activates DHEA. When you have more DHEA, your heart rhythm gets more coherent and you are emotionally resilient; the app registers green or blue. If your body releases more cortisol due to negative emotions, your heart rhythm becomes noncoherent, and the app shows red.

We keep a funny doll called Tickle Me Elmo on the range at VISION54 schools. When students see the Elmo doll, they can't help but laugh. If you have your sensor on, you'll see your emotions move the sensor into the green or blue zone. Elmo is an external object that creates positive emotions and DHEA. External objects can also create negative emotions and cortisol. If you get angry at a poor shot, you'll probably see your sensor move into the red. By playing a round with the sensor, you can see how you respond in real situations on the course. You learn how to self-regulate; you can consciously calm yourself and create positive emotions. You can increase your adrenaline and create more DHEA. This makes emotional resilience more than just a concept. Once you begin to understand the feedback, you can remove the device and create the feelings on your own. It makes emotional management and resilience a real human skill.

When we started working with Suzann Pettersen in 2006, she began using the HeartMath app. At first, she couldn't get it out of the red zone at all. By March 2007, her work with the app had enabled her to start shifting her emotions. She never really told us what feelings she was activating to make it turn green, but she was clearly getting more in touch with her inner awareness. We don't know whether it was an accident or not that 2007 was the best year of her career. We think not.

In early 2016, when Ariya Jutanugarn came to us for coaching, she had developed a specific terror of hitting her driver off the tee, and a general fear of performing badly in tournaments. Working with the handheld HeartMath app, she was able to see where, when, and why the sensor went to red and, conversely, to green and blue. For the first time, she learned how she could create a different emotional state before stepping into her shot. She now had a skill, something practical she could do to shift from a worried anxiety state to a happier and more joyous state.

To sum up: The most important piece of equipment in golf is your body, with its mind, emotions, and physical coordination. HeartMath is a simple tool that has provided golfers both the insight and the means to help manage our emotional states.

BEFORE, DURING, AND AFTER THE ROUND

YOUR HUMAN INVENTORY

PEOPLE OFTEN ASK US, "What professional players do you have in your coaching stable?" We answer, "We're sorry, but we don't have a stable. We have a harbor. Players sail into the harbor to take our VISION54 programs, and to work on their games and human skills. Our goal is for them to sail out, knowing they can always manage themselves on the golf course. They know where our harbor is, but they are the captains of their own ships."

So far, we have explored human skills of awareness, variability, balance, tempo, and tension; we have created our boxes— Think Box, Play Box, and Memory Box; and we have explored how we can regulate the body, mind, and emotions between shots on the course.

Now it's time to put these things together, to understand what you do best (and worst) on the course, and to create a unique (and flexible) game plan for a round that matters—whether it's your club championship or a tournament. Your game plan will give you the tools to clearly evaluate your play after a round.

CHAPTER 10

MASTER OF VARIABILITY:
MY54 AND NOT54

MOST GOLFERS KNOW A LOT about what they do when they play badly. They'll say, "I three-putted six holes today," or "I couldn't hit my drives," or "I didn't have the right distance on my pitch shots," or "I just got down on myself." Knowing what went wrong on the course is necessary. But it's equally important, if not more important, to know what went right—and why.

One of the most valuable things you can do for your game is to start recording what you do when you play well, and when you don't play well. What were you aware of when you were swinging the club? What did you notice when you were putting? What did you do, or feel, between shots? What kind of self-talk did you have? Were you more introverted or extroverted? How well did you commit to your decisions? Was your adrenaline low or high?

These are what we call your MY54 and NOT54 inventories. MY54 and NOT54 are your unique maps of how you play— physically, mentally, and emotionally. The list includes the signature ways you play your best, and how you usually mess up on the course. It doesn't matter if you're a 36-handicap or a professional—all of us have our MY54s and NOT54s. Most of us experience a combination of both during the same round. They tend to be consistent.

Unfortunately, most golfers still have the mind-set that they're supposed to achieve consistency, and when they don't, something is wrong (usually with their technique). Players tend to focus on what they do badly on the course, rather than what they do well. Remember the concept of variability, the principle that nothing is the same from shot to shot, hole to hole, round to round, and day to day? Remember our 3:1 negativity bias— that we store negative memories three times more powerfully than positive memories? So it shouldn't be surprising that we know more about what goes wrong with our games than what goes right. The more clearly you understand the elements of your MY54 and NOT54, your strengths and weaknesses, the more frequently you'll be able to catch yourself "mid-screwup" (hopefully before an error becomes a disaster or a full-blown meltdown) and begin to counteract it by dialing in your human skills. This ability will make you a Master of Variability.

We want you to be clued-in about your golf game, instead of clue-less. Instead of sitting in the bar after the round, hearing your playing partner say to you, "After the 10th hole, you started swinging too fast, and that's when you started missing all those shots," we want you to have recognized it yourself, then stepped onto the 11th tee with the thought, *My NOT54 fast tempo is beginning to show up, so I'm going to swing at 60 percent on this next hole.* When you can do that, you're a player.

The origins of MY54 and NOT54 date back to the early 1990s, when Pia started following her Swedish national team players onto the course and observing them while they played. She noticed that some played better when they were extroverted and chatty, and others played better when they were introverted and quiet. She watched how the players made decisions on the course. "I observed their pre-shot routines, their swings, basically everything I could," says Pia. "I'd say to one player, 'Here's what I noticed on holes 4, 5, and 6, when you were playing great. Here's what I saw on holes 16 and 17, when you weren't playing so well.'" While both good and bad processes manifest in technique, they are often caused by other factors, internal and external variables, at a given moment.

One day, Pia wrote up her observations for a player in a short report, because she wasn't going to be able to see her after her tournament round. Soon she was writing notes for all the players. Some had to do with their pace of play and the time they spent over the ball. Often when they were playing well, they kept a certain pace, and when they weren't playing well, they would stand over the ball longer, overpreparing for shots, or distracted while swinging. Pia was fascinated by all the things she observed before, during, and after their shots. She picked up on whether a player knew how to make a proper drop near a water hazard or how he or she was interacting with a playing partner. She thought, *Wow, if I were still on tour, these would be really good things to know.*

As we do with all the ideas that are part of VISION54, we personally tested the concepts of MY54 and NOT54. Pia found that, when she plays well, she's deeply present in her Play Box. "My most important MY54 is to feel something in my body. When I'm playing my best, I feel calm, with a low center of gravity and even tempo. When all of that is in sync, I'm clear about what actions to take. I don't think about scoring or winning. I feel totally present and free. And I play without expectations."

Lynn's MY54s relate to being present in her Play Box, too. "I focus on having a soft, wide visual connection to the target, and on a feeling of wholeness with my swing from takeaway to finish. I also like to be social between shots. It keeps me relaxed. And I love the feeling of connection to nature."

Pia's NOT54s include her tempo, letting her mind go to the future, and worrying about things that haven't even happened. For Lynn, her NOT54s include her grip pressure getting tight, which makes her clubface shut. "Emotionally, one of my NOT54s is getting stuck in the past, thinking about something I didn't like on a previous hole, and then kind of obsessing on it. From there, I get grumpy."

We've interviewed many of the great players of the game about their MY54s. Most of them know exactly what they did when they played their best. JoAnne Carner is a World Golf Hall of Famer who won 43 times on the LPGA Tour. JoAnne didn't turn pro until she was 30, and at age 65, she was still playing in LPGA tournaments (she holds the record for being the oldest player in history to make the cut in a professional event). JoAnne told us: "I closed the door on the last shot very quickly and moved on to the next one. If my caddie asked me, 'Did you pull that putt?' I would answer, 'What putt? I'm on a new hole now.'"

Gary Player, the South African who won nine major championships during his career and was the third player in history (and the first non-American) to win the career Grand Slam, said, "It was my short memory and my ability to handle adversity."

Nancy Lopez, who won 48 tournaments and three majors during her 24-year career, told us: "I was always positive. I learned that from my dad. If I hit a bad shot, he would tell me, 'The next shot might be the best one you've ever hit.' I was never negative on the golf course."

And Tom Weiskopf, who won 16 PGA Tour titles before becoming an acclaimed golf course architect, shared, "It was

always my tempo and balance, and sensing speed in putting."
As you might notice, these MY54s have more to do with performance states than with technical swing details. These are human skills: the ability to focus and access sensory "feelings" of balance, tempo, and distance perception, and the ability to stay positive and put negative thoughts out of your mind.

Identifying and building your MY54 and NOT54 lists is one of the most important things you can do for your game. At our VISION54 schools, we ask our students after each session: "What did you do when you played your best today? What did you do when you didn't play so well? What did you do between holes? We want all of you to start building your awareness muscles, and to keep refining them." Because of our natural 3:1 negativity bias, we ask players to start by listing three MY54s and one NOT54—reversing the bias from negative to positive. Pick just one common NOT54. The more MY54s you can put on your list, the better.

Here are a few MY54 and NOT54 examples from players with whom we've worked. Annika Sorenstam's MY54s were her simple approach; her total commitment to her decisions; being present for each shot; focus on her process (rather than on things outside her control); her short four-to-five-second Play Box; her awareness of what was happening internally and externally; and her discipline in managing it. Annika's best MY54 was her courage in being honest. She didn't resort to blame or excuses; she aimed for balance in her golf and in her life.

Russell Knox's MY54s are his confidence and clarity stepping into his Play Box; his strong body language; excellent balance at the finish of his swing; management of his self-talk; mastery of his Memory Box (especially with his "good enough" shots); and trust in his gut or intuition, especially on the greens.

Kevin Streelman's MY54s are his grit (he never gives up); his ability to see his ball flight; his awareness and management of his grip pressure and swing tempo; his belief in his swing; his ability to create DHEA and enjoyment on the course; his life perspective based on his faith; and his work ethic and gratitude.

At the end of the first day of our three-day VISION54 schools, we ask our students to begin identifying their MY54s. At one of our programs, Eric, a filmmaker from Los Angeles, identified one of his MY54s as walking onto the tee feeling balanced and confident. Zach, a 1-handicap, told us one of his MY54s was when his swing tempo was about 80 percent. Mia, a college golfer, said her MY54 was chatting with her playing partners and smiling.

It's great when more of your MY54s are showing up during a round, but what happens when your NOT54s begin to intrude? Quickly recognizing them is important. If you catch them, you can initiate a "shift" back to your MY54s. Shifting isn't difficult, but many players forget to do it, because they get caught up in the outcome of the shot and its aftermath (see Russell Knox at the Players Championship). This is why we tell our players: Write one, two, or three of your most important MY54s down on your scorecard, in your notebook, on your glove, or wherever you can take a quick glance to remind yourself during the round. Kristine, one of our VISION54 coaches, keeps a card with her MY54s in her bag. If she loses focus during a match or isn't hitting the ball the way she likes, she pulls out the card and refreshes herself. "It helps me reset," she says. "I'm usually able to play better right away."

Arron Oberholser says his NOT54s would kick in right away

when he hit a bad shot. His NOT54s were a "poor-me" attitude, low adrenaline, negative emotions, and cortisol buildup. We worked with him on how to shift back to his MY54s. When he hit a poor shot, he would spend one or two minutes before his next shot feeling positive emotions, so his body would start accessing DHEA, and he would engage in positive self-talk as he walked up the fairway. "I would say to myself, *Show me what a great shot looks like, Arron. Show me how good you are,*" he says.

The skill of shifting from NOT54 to MY54 is critical. It's catching yourself mid-screwup. You'll never be able to create a situation on the range that replicates this series of events, which is why it's so important to practice on the course. Only by exploring these tools in the context of your game can you find out what works—which "shifts" work best for you at which times. It might be that you need to change something in your Think Box, Play Box, or Memory Box. It might require a shift in your physical, mental, or emotional state.

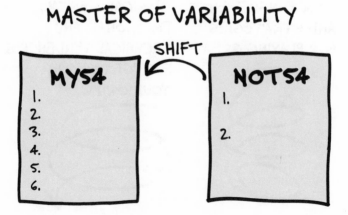

The idea is to access an upward spiral in your performance state and game; MY54 actions make that more likely to happen. All of us hit a downward spiral at some point on the course. The goal is to catch your NOT54 early and be able to shift it before the climb back to neutral becomes too steep. One of the best examples of shifting we've observed was at the PGA Tour's Tampa Bay Championship in 2013. Kevin Streelman was leading the tournament. If he won, it would be his first PGA Tour victory. He was walking from the 17th to the 18th hole, and he could feel his adrenaline and nervousness spiking. He knew his swing tempo would speed up with this higher adrenaline, so he consciously shifted to a Play Box feel of 30–40 percent swing tempo. He managed his shots perfectly on the 18th hole, and won his first PGA Tour tournament.

MY54
EACH PLAYER'S
UNIQUE INGREDIENTS
AND STRATEGIES
FOR PLAYING GREAT

NOT54
EACH PLAYER'S
PHYSICAL, MENTAL,
EMOTIONAL, AND
TECHNICAL TENDENCIES
FOR "GETTING IN
YOUR OWN WAY"

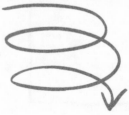

Another player we've worked with who benefitted enormously from MY54 and NOT54 management is LPGA Tour veteran Brittany Lang, who won the 2016 U.S. Women's Open at CordeValle Golf Club near San Martin, California. (The win made Brittany the first golfer to win the U.S. Open at 30 or older since 36-year-old Annika Sorenstam in 2006.)

Brittany came to see us early in 2008. She'd been on the LPGA Tour for about two years and had six top-10 finishes. Like Suzann Pettersen, she felt she was underperforming—and didn't know why. Brittany had been a champion junior golfer. She won eight American Junior Golf Association (AJGA) events, was a member of the PING Junior Solheim Cup team, and at Duke University, she was an All-American and a member of the U.S. Curtis Cup team that beat Great Britain and Ireland in 2004. Brittany qualified for her first U.S. Women's Open at Cherry Hills in Denver in 2005 as an amateur (the same tournament where Lorena Ochoa put her drive into the water on 18). Brittany was just 20 years old and nearly won the tournament, tying for second place with another promising amateur, Morgan Pressel. Brittany turned professional in July 2005, and qualified for the LPGA Tour in 2006.

The moment we met her, we could tell that one of her strongest MY54s was her clear, simple style of play. She's a natural athlete. She's hardworking. She doesn't worry too much about her technique. She plays the game with a positive attitude and positive self-talk. She carries herself with great body language.

At the time, Brittany had a coach who was urging her to be more technical and statistic-focused. Because she's such an intuitive, feel player, we could tell that she was being drawn away from her natural style of play.

"When I was young, I remember I had this little voice inside my head that tried to infiltrate my thoughts. I would obsess about score or technique, or what wasn't going well," she says. "I was able to put it out of my mind when I was a junior, which was awesome. Everything seemed simple. Then I turned professional, and I started listening to that voice. Even worse, I started believing it. I felt totally at odds with myself."

One of the first things we did with Brittany was have her identify the MY54s in her game that were truest to who she was—and the ones that produced her best golf. She settled on an acronym she called QDANT: Quick, Decisive, Aggressive, No Thoughts. "BTG" was the MY54 nickname she gave herself: Brittany The Great. We loved it.

Over the years, her focus on simplicity and her MY54s worked well for her. But she felt she could play better. So five years later, in 2013, she sailed back into our VISION54 harbor. She said she felt she was getting too complicated in her Think Box. It was confusing her decision-making, and making her unclear about her commitment in her Play Box. Her attention was unfocused; she'd lost the feeling of connectedness and awareness in her body.

Understanding that players are always refining their MY54s on the course, we suggested she go out and play nine holes without any Think Box whatsoever, using only instinct to decide on her shots. She called us afterward and said she was amazed at how well she had played. She felt free and crystal-clear when she was hitting the ball. Afterward, she decided to de-clutter her brain even more. She stopped carrying her own yardage book during tournaments and asked her caddie (also her brother), Luke, to give her specific yardage information.

We talked with Brittany about how to keep refreshing her MY54s. A more visual Play Box resonated with her. "As a kid, I just looked at the target and played," she says. "Over time, I got away from that. Now I'm back to connecting with my target, seeing my ball flight to the flag, and staying with the image of the shot until I finish my swing. When I putt, I like to hear the sound of the ball going into the cup. Those are the MY54s that really help me to stay engaged. If I commit to them, I can hit great shot after great shot. The other thing I worked on was MY54 attitude. I practiced letting go of my bad shots. I got back to the even-keeled, positive attitude I'd always had. Right now, my attitude is one of the greatest strengths of my game."

Brittany found dependable ways to shift from NOT54 to MY54. "On days when I'm seeing more NOT54s than MY54s in my game, I have a tendency to say to myself, *Shoot, I play so good when I can see the shot going to the target, but today it's not working.* So I tell myself over and over, *See the target and commit to what you're doing—all the way to the finish.* And by 'all the way to the finish,' I mean all the way to the finish of each swing, and all the way to the finish of the round. That simple idea is a huge thing for me."

Brittany adds, "It's about finding resources on the days you don't have your A game. That's usually when I didn't get enough sleep, and I'm tired. Once when I was playing in Canada, even though I had made a bunch of pars, I was feeling lethargic. My Play Box wasn't clear. I told myself, *Brittany, you need to build some DHEA energy and good feeling. On every hole on the back nine, think of at least one thing you're grateful for that makes you happy.* On one hole, I would think about having a really nice dinner with my husband, Kevin. The next hole, I'd think about my little puppy, or how blessed I am. All of a sudden, my Play Box became super, super clear. I'll never forget that day. I think I shot 5-under on the back nine. I was able to make the shift from NOT54 to MY54."

Brittany credits these human skills for her U.S. Women's Open victory in 2016. "I needed them more than ever to stay in my process," she says. "Two ideas that really worked for me on the course during the Open were 'good pictures' and 'good commitment.' They were my focus that week. On the back nine on Sunday—it was hole 12—I hit a really, really good iron shot. I'd had a great picture of it in my head. I had good commitment. I held my finish. I did everything I wanted to do, but I think I had a little too much adrenaline going, and I hit it over the green into a bunker. I stayed super calm and super relaxed. I was like, *No big deal. I can get this up and down.* I had a great picture in my head of my bunker shot, and great commitment. I got up and down. That's BTG54—no complaining, no whining, just full commitment."

On the next hole, the par-4 13th, Brittany hit her second shot, a 9-iron, onto the green and 50 feet from the pin. "I was so confident I was going to make that putt," she says. "It was going nowhere but into the hole. I felt it and saw it. I birdied the hole."

SUMMING UP HER TOURNAMENT, Brittany says, "I stayed 'inner.' I didn't look outside the ropes. I didn't look at the leaderboard. Between each shot, I was singing to myself or feeling my feet in my shoes or thinking about things I'm grateful for. I was building DHEA during the entire round each day, and not thinking about outcomes. The rest took care of itself."

Our VISION54 work with MY54 and NOT54 eventually

got us thinking some more. If you know what your NOT54 tendencies are—maybe you get too fast with your tempo, or start thinking too much about outcomes—why can't you be *proactive* during a round to eliminate or reduce your NOT54s before they even show up? If you know that your tendency is to get ahead of yourself—worrying about making the cut in a tournament or shooting a certain score—why not practice breathing or looking at the trees between shots, or every three holes, bringing yourself into the present before trouble starts? We started testing this with a few players and found that it works, effectively expanding the physical, mental, and emotional recharge we discussed in previous chapters.

The reality of golf is that you're the one holding the club and hitting the ball. YOU are the expert on you. Awareness will give you new insights into the issues that show up in your technique. More and more, you will understand the connection on the golf course. MY54 and NOT54 are the means to see yourself clearly—no side mirrors.

THE CRUCIAL INVENTORY: MY54, NOT54

ALL OF US HAVE SIGNATURE WAYS that we play our best golf. MY54 is like a fingerprint; it's *who we are* and *what we do.* No one else has the same MY54. No one else has the same NOT54.

If you're going to bake a cake of great golf, you need to know what ingredients go into the cake. Begin to build your MY54 ingredient list. After you play a round, say to yourself, *I played those three holes really well. What did I do on those holes?* Keep a *Be a Player* notebook and make observations about your game for a month. If your MY54 ingredients are "I was confident. I was relaxed. I was happy," those are not specific enough. You need to drill it down to *how* you experienced confidence, *how* you experienced relaxation, and *how* you experienced happiness. Where did you feel those sensations in your body? What were the states of your mind and emotions? For another person, the MY54 ingredients might include strong body language between shots, committing to decisions, and maintaining constant grip pressure. Again, drill it down further. How do these manifest in your body, your brain, and your emotions? The ingredients are the basics—your flour, sugar, eggs, and water. How much did you need of each to perform at your best? The more detailed you can make your MY54 list, the better the cake.

MY54, NOT54: QUESTIONS

MY54:

- What are you aware of during your best swings and strokes?
- How do your body, mind, and emotions feel between your best shots?
- How do you react to your best shots?
- What shots do you most like to hit, and what is your general course strategy?
- Are you generally in the past, present, or future when you're playing? When do you play your best?
- Are you quiet, or do you like to talk to yourself or others between shots?

- What is your adrenaline level when you play your best?

- What do you eat and drink during your best rounds?

- What tension level do you notice in your body when you play well?

- What tempo is best for you?

- How do you make decisions for each shot during a good round?

- How is your commitment when you play your best?

- What's good about your technique during a good or great round?

- What can you do to access your MY54 list more often before you play?

- What can you do to access your MY54s when you are on the course?

MY54

1. WHAT DO YOU DO WHEN YOU ENJOY PLAYING?
  ○ _____
  ○ _____

3. WHO ARE YOU BEING?
  ○ _____
  ○ _____
  ○ _____

1.
2.
3.
4.

2. WHAT DO YOU DO WHEN YOU PLAY YOUR BEST?
  ○ _____
  ○ _____

4. HOW DO YOU FEEL? THINK?
  ○ _____
  ○ _____

NOT54:

- How do you usually get in your own way on the golf course?

- What happens in your Think Box, Play Box, and Memory Box when you don't play well?

- What is the technical part of your game that goes awry when you play poorly?

- What do you do between shots when your game isn't at its best?

- What situations tend to make your NOT54s appear?

- What's most important for you to be aware of to catch your NOT54s early?

What tools can help you shift from your NOT54s to MY54s?

MY54, NOT54: ON-COURSE EXPLORATIONS

PLAY NINE HOLES and explore one of these exercises on each hole.

1. On one hole, pay attention to the top three things you do when you are playing great golf.

2. On one hole, see, feel, and hear a great Play Box before you hit each shot.

3. On one hole, give yourself bad lies on each shot, and see how well you can manage yourself.

4. On one hole, pause between each shot for 30 seconds, and imagine your body, mind, and emotions being in the best state possible.

5. On one hole, choose a shot or club you normally don't like, and see how well you can manage yourself.

6. On one hole, imagine that your group is lagging behind, and you need to play faster to catch up. Play extra fast, but still get into a good state when it's your turn to hit a shot.

7. On one hole, create the one thing you do most when you get in your own way (swinging too fast, doubting your decision, getting tight in your shoulders, etc.).

8. On one hole, decide what you want to pay attention to before each shot, so you can shift into your MY54 state again.

9. On one hole, pick one thing on your MY54 list and feel it more strongly than you ever have before.

NOT54

1. WHAT CAN YOU DO TO SHIFT TO MY54?

o _____
o _____
o _____
o _____
o _____
o _____

1.

2.

2. WHAT DO YOU DO DIFFERENTLY WHEN YOU GET IN YOUR OWN WAY?

o _____
o _____
o _____
o _____
o _____
o _____

LYNN: THE HUMAN POTENTIAL
OF MICHAEL MURPHY

MOST GOLFERS KNOW Michael Murphy for his novel *Golf in the Kingdom*. It tells the story of Michael Murphy, a young man who goes to live on an ashram in India. On his way home, Michael stops in Scotland, and decides to play a round of golf at Burningbush, a famous golf course. There he bumps into a mystical guru named Shivas Irons, who teaches him about golf and spirituality.

Pia and I read *Golf in the Kingdom* independently when we were in our 20s. One of my mentors, Tom Shea, had encouraged me to read it, and another mentor, Chuck Hogan, practically lived by the book. In my view, Tom and Chuck were American versions of Shivas Irons. Both Pia and I were fascinated that there was a side of golf that was so mystical and full of potential.

Michael Murphy co-founded the Esalen Institute in Big Sur, California, in 1962, with his good friend Dick Price. Esalen was a place where people from different domains came together to discuss how they might work toward achieving something called human potential. Michael is also a scholar of philosophy and metaphysics who studies extraordinary capacities in human beings and how we can make "the extraordinary" a part of our lives—including our golf games.

When Pia and I started coaching together, we went to Esalen

for a few days. Shortly afterward, we attended a PGA Teaching and Coaching Summit in New Orleans. Lo and behold, Michael Murphy was one of the speakers! Even though we'd never met him, we decided to write him a note to tell him how much he'd inspired us. We left the note under the door of his hotel room.

About a year later, we decided to organize a coaching seminar of our own at the Legacy Golf Resort in Phoenix. Crazily, we said, "Let's invite Michael Murphy to come speak to our group." When we contacted him, he said, "Of course. You're the two ladies who slipped that nice note under my door in New Orleans. I know about your work, and I'd love to talk to your coaches."

We were shocked—and elated. Before the seminar, we had a telephone conversation with him. We asked, "What do you think is stopping golfers from shooting 54?" He didn't pause. He said, "That's easy. It's distraction."

By distraction, he meant that golfers weren't totally present—to themselves or their games. As human beings, he said, golfers don't stay with what they're doing long enough or deeply enough.

Michael and his colleague Andy Nussbaum arrived for the day-long training with our coaches. They said to our group, "Give us words or phrases that describe how you feel when you play your best golf." The coaches spoke, and Michael and Andy wrote down their words on the board: *Calm, out of my mind, relaxed, centered, time stood still, confident, like an out-of-body experience, ultra-easy, I didn't have to do anything, the target looked huge, and close, I could do anything with the golf ball.*

Later, Michael asked us if any golf teachers worked on these ideas and feelings with their students, or if most taught "angles and elbows." He said golfers would never achieve peak performance by practicing technique alone. Most people use only a fraction of our human capacities, he said, and he challenged Pia and me to create an environment where golfers could learn about and access their full abilities. He told us that these abilities were previously hidden, implicit, untouchable, and reputed to be the exclusive provenance of legendary athletes who were born with mysterious abilities. Michael not only insisted this wasn't true, he gave us our most ambitious assignment: "Make the implicit explicit," he urged us.

That day, Michael taught all the coaches how to meditate and explained that meditation is a common human activity, and that you can meditate with your eyes open, which is what happens when golfers or other athletes enter "the zone." Together, we did a walking meditation from one side of the range to the other. Afterward, we did what you might call a "swinging" meditation, in which people tried to stay in a calm, quiet state while swinging the club. Nobody was allowed to talk.

In his book *The Future of the Body*, Michael argues that to be human is to have the potential for the extraordinary. "Superfluid," "peak performance," "flow," or "in the zone" states are neither mysterious nor mystical, he says, but normal human capacities. Ancient practitioners of hatha yoga in India had tremendous mastery of their autonomic nervous systems, he explained—able to control their breathing and heart rates, some of the very things that HeartMath teaches now. Michael likens sports to a 21st-century version of yoga, in which athletes learn to slip into and out of alpha and theta brainwave states as easily as they slip into and out of their shoes.

Michael believes that development of our extraordinary capacities is part of the next phase of human evolution, and that a new kind of teaching is necessary to bring these capacities to fruition. Once we access our sensory-motor abilities more deeply, extremely advanced skills can emerge. There is a "psychic side of sports," he says, and many athletes (and other performers) can access profound dimensions of themselves that translate into extraordinary performances.

Golf instruction has historically been about "faults and fixes" and teacher-centered learning. Michael encouraged us to engage in a new approach of cultivating awareness, asking open-ended questions, listening to our students—as well as continuing to be students of disciplines other than golf.

We stay in touch with Michael and have visited him during the past few years outside San Francisco, where he lives. He's in his mid-80s now, and he's as active and curious as ever. We love that Michael introduced us to the idea of the "supernormal" in every golfer. And we love these words he wrote in his book *On the Edge of the Future*: "I had this feeling that we all had access to the ground of being, or God, or light. Our job in life was to get in touch with it, and to bring it into the world through meditation, friendship, prayer, music, and even sports."

As Michael would say, *Om*.

CHAPTER 11

YOUR HUMAN-SKILLS
GAME PLAN

A FRIEND OF OURS was playing in a summer-long match play tournament at her club. One day, she asked several of her fellow golfers, "Do any of you make a game plan for your upcoming matches?" The players, whose handicaps ranged from 10 to 36, looked at her with curiosity.

"Well, I usually know how many strokes I'm either going to give to or get from my opponent—so I know where my opportunities are," one said.

"I don't think that much about it," said another. "It all comes down to putting, anyway."

For 95 percent of golfers, we'd say this is the extent of thinking about a game plan. Recently, we decided to conduct our own test. We stood near the first tee and asked golfers, "What are each of your game plans? What are you going to focus on today?" One person said, "I'm going to try to lower my handicap." Another laughed, "I'm just going to focus on winning." And a third said, "I'll try to play my best."

Notice how vague and general their game plans were. It's interesting to compare them to those of a PGA Tour or LPGA Tour player, who is usually highly specific about his or her game plan and focus. Brittany Lang's game plan before the U.S. Women's Open was to stay within herself and not look outside the ropes, or at the leaderboard. She focused on sensations such as sound (singing to herself) or feel (her feet inside her shoes). She created happy feelings during each round to build DHEA. In press conferences after a professional tournament round, a player will say, "I decided on my game plan before the tournament, and I'm proud that I stayed committed to it through all four rounds." What they're talking about is their process, the particular things on which they will focus. The external conditions will change during a round (and a tournament), but the game plan remains the same.

Most golfers have, at best, a one-dimensional game plan. If a part of their game begins to falter—they start slicing the ball or missing the green with their pitch and chip shots—they usually react to the last shot and blame their technique. We don't blame people for this default tendency. They haven't learned anything else. The most glaring blind spot in most golfers' games, the biggest missing piece, is the ability to identify what is going on and to manage themselves on the course.

VISION54, and this book, are about adding a different set of skills and a different game plan to your repertoire. It's a *proactive* plan that acknowledges variability, allowing you to manage what's actually under your control. The word "process" gets thrown around a lot in golf instruction. People get confused by it, because they think process is a concept, not something real. We believe that human skills *are* your process. We've named them so they are clear: awareness of your physical, mental, and emotional states; commitment to your Think Box, Play Box, and Memory Box; keeping in touch with your balance, tempo, and tension; managing your self-talk; understanding your MY54s and NOT54s (and shifting when your NOT54s show up); and practicing emotional resilience. Executing these particular skills means staying in your process. This is your game plan.

Brittany Lang flawlessly executed her game plan when she won the U.S. Women's Open. "I stuck to my MY54," she says. "I was quick, aggressive, and decisive, no thought. The two things that I concentrated on were 'good pictures'—that is, visualizing my shots—and 'good commitment to my decisions and Play Box.' I did those really, really well."

Before we get to the specifics of how to create your own human-skills game plan, we'd like to tell you a story. In 2014, Kevin Streelman had missed four cuts in a row before arriving at the U.S. Open at Pinehurst. Kevin has always been a good ball-striker, but he wasn't hitting the ball well. He was frustrated and upset. At the time, he was also working with his swing coach, who wanted him to make some technical changes. Kevin didn't feel comfortable with what his coach was recommending, but they'd been together for so long that he went along with his recommendations.

We arrived at Pinehurst a few days before the tournament and followed Kevin for some of the practice and tournament rounds. We watched him struggle. After the second round of the Open, we sat down to talk with him outside the clubhouse and next to the croquet courts, in the scorching-hot North Carolina sun. We talked for several hours, and barely noticed the heat.

"One of the biggest things I took away from that conversation was a question Lynn asked me," Kevin recalls. "She said, 'Kevin, if you were coaching yourself, what would you say about your golf swing right now?'

"For five to 10 minutes I told Lynn everything I didn't like about my swing," Kevin says, recalling the conversation. "The gist of what my coach was telling me was that he wanted the club back deep in my swing, pretty far behind me. I felt the club was too far inside, getting shut on the backswing, and getting stuck coming down."

Kevin told us he knew he wanted the club in front of his chest, so he could make his turn with a square clubface. It was a pretty clear-cut technique issue. Finally, Lynn said, "Kevin, this is *your* swing. This is *your* profession. Why are you allowing another person, even your coach, to override your best instincts?"

"It really hit me," says Kevin. "I'd been avoiding confronting what was right in front of me."

Kevin missed the cut at Pinehurst. But he was already in a better place. He traveled to Washington, D.C., after the tournament, where he talked with a swing instructor with whom he felt more in sync. Then he went on to the next tournament, the Travelers Championship at TPC River Highlands in Connecticut.

He texted us that he felt much better—and that he had made the cut. All of a sudden, things started to get special for him on the weekend. He hit the ball just the way he wanted to on Saturday, and shot a 64. In the final round on Sunday, he made the turn with a 36, including two bogeys and a birdie. Then he started an amazing run, one-putting on holes 9, 10, and 11. Like a Formula One car easing into lower and more efficient gears, Kevin birdied the last seven holes—breaking the PGA Tour record for consecutive closing birdies by a winner. He won the tournament with a 7-under 28 on the final nine, shooting another 64.

"It will probably go down as one of the top one or two rounds of my career," he says. "And it never would've happened without that conversation I had with Pia and Lynn at Pinehurst. I started focusing on my mental outlook, on my belief structure, and on being in charge of my own game plan. I took control of myself and went from pretty much the lowest I'd ever felt in my professional career to the highest within a couple of weeks."

Brittany Lang went through something similar in the process of becoming her own best coach. Several years ago, she had started working with a swing instructor who she felt, again, was too technical for her game. This time, she decided to split with the coach and to manage herself with the help of her brother and caddie, Luke. "At first, I was nervous that I didn't have a coach," she says. "I was on my own. In one way, it was really cool to go out and play nine holes and not have to listen to anybody. But now I was the one who had to decide what to work on."

Brittany was out of our VISION54 harbor during this period. Now she says, "Ironically, it wasn't until I stopped working with Pia and Lynn that I started to see more clearly the importance of the human skills they teach. I sat down and said, 'Okay, well, I'm not going to do anything with my swing, because I have a great natural swing. Then I thought, *Okay, Brittany, what do you need to do to play your best?* I realized I had to go more inward to play well. I'd worked with Pia and Lynn and VISION54 long enough to know that I needed to strengthen my commitment to my decisions and my shots. I knew I needed to constantly be creating DHEA on the course. I knew I needed to guard against creating cortisol. On some level, this is simple, basic stuff. But like everything else, it takes discipline and practice. When I'm on the range now, I commit to every single shot I hit. I'm working on a good Play Box, on balance, tempo, and tension. I am never just *hitting a ball.*"

So now it's time. You're about to play in your club championship or a member-guest tournament, or a regional or national
USGA competition, or a mini-tour event or a PGA or LPGA
Tour tournament. You need to create your game plan. Yes, it
might include general strategy for each hole, if you're playing
stroke play or match play—these are external factors. Now, we
want you to add your own specific human-skills game plan.
It'll be the summary of the essential things that you want to
pay attention to before a shot, during a shot, after a shot, and
between shots. You've learned about the human skills in this
book; now we want you to personalize them for yourself. The
game plan includes your MY54 and NOT54 tendencies and
the tools to shift from NOT54 to MY54. Before you head out
to the course, think about the few most important things you
want to pay attention to today. Depending on how you feel, is it
your tempo? Might it be remembering to keep calm by taking
deep breaths? Is it to be okay with "good enough" shots and
processes? The things you decide on will become your game
plan and playing focus for the day.

People often ask us, "Do professional players ever need help
making game plans?" We chuckle, because professionals need
help with game plans just as much as amateurs.

When we're at tournaments with our professional players,
we make sure that they are clear about the day's game plan and
the playing focus. It's not a laundry list. It might be 75-percent
tempo in their Play Box, and to loosen their hips every three
holes. It might be a constant grip pressure with a balanced posture. If they're feeling a slight lack of confidence, they might
make sure their body language is extra strong between holes.

The warm-up before an important round is part of your

game plan. It's not mindlessly hitting shots on the range, hoping to feel one pure strike before you tee off. It's not a practice session to improve your skills or fix something in your swing at the last minute. We like to call it Intentional Warm-Up. The purpose is to warm up your body, mind, and emotions. You will warm up your balance, tempo, and tension so you can step onto the first tee with confidence. The first thing is to check in with yourself on the day of competition. Who am I today? How am I feeling? How are my physical, mental, and emotional states? Is there anything I need to pay extra attention to today? Am I nervous, sluggish, extra-tight in my shoulders, off balance, or worried about things outside of golf?

Russell Knox starts with balance exercises, hitting balls on one leg, then the other, on the practice range. Brittany Lang listens to music on her headphones to get relaxed. Other players practice extremely slow "tai-chi" swings with their eyes closed to access inner awareness of their swings. Kevin Streelman hits balls with a slow tempo in his warm-up, gradually increasing the speed to his normal tempo.

Next, decide on the playing focus you'll commit to for the day.

I'm going to pay extra attention to my grip pressure.

I'm going to use 80-percent tempo.

I'm playing with people who are quiet, and I like to talk, so I need to sing songs in my head or talk to imaginary friends between shots.

I'm nervous today, so I will take deep breaths between shots to calm myself down.

Ai Miyazato, an LPGA Tour player we've worked with for many years, used to carry a special "playing focus" scorecard during her tournament rounds. The first time she did this, her caddie said he couldn't figure out what she was doing. She hit her drive into a bunker on one hole. In his opinion, it wasn't a good drive, but Ai wrote down a 5 (on a scale of 1 to 5, with 5 being best). Later, she made a long putt and wrote down a 3. He couldn't figure out the correlation. After the round, she told him, "I was keeping track of how committed I stayed to my decisions. The numbers weren't about outcome." Commitment to her shots was the main skill that Ai worked on strengthening. During 2010, she held the World No. 1 ranking for 12 consecutive weeks.

Ariya Jutanugarn learned that she needed to adjust her game plan during a tournament round in response to increasing levels of pressure and stress. At the 2016 ANA Inspiration, the year's first major, she was leading by two strokes on Sunday with three holes to play. With her first major win in her grasp, she bogeyed the final three holes to finish fourth.

Ariya hadn't realized how much her internal states were changing in response to stress, so she'd continued with her same Play Box feels during the final three holes, thinking they would work for her. They didn't. After the tournament, we talked it over together, and she came up with an additional Play Box strategy. The next time she was close to winning and feeling pressure, she decided to take *more* deep breaths to release tension, get *more present* to her Play Box feel before she entered it, and *commit even more strongly* to the shot, going deeper into her Play Box focus and creating even more DHEA.

When Suzann Pettersen put her game plan into play during the 2007 LPGA Championship, she focused on not overthinking her shots and on maintaining her emotional resilience. She kept her Play Box under 10 seconds, she walked with her head up, and she conducted herself with positive body language and energy off the tee. She reminded herself to relax her jaw and talk to her caddie between shots, and she closed the door efficiently on shots she had just hit. The result: Her first victory in a major.

GOOD? BETTER? HOW? ——>ACTION

LPGA player Yani Tseng's game plan for her final round at the Women's British Open at Royal Birkdale in 2010 was related to a drop in confidence and negative self-talk. She kept her Play Box to five seconds, maintained strong body language when walking down the fairways, and sang Taiwanese children's songs to distract herself between shots to keep her mind from jumping to outcome. That outcome, by the way, was that she won the tournament, becoming the first women's player in the modern era to win five major championships.

Russell Knox's game plan that led to his first win at the WGC-HSBC in Shanghai in 2015 was to visualize his shots, keep his Think Box simple, and trust his instincts. He kept his Play Box short; focused on his balance, tempo, and tension; and made sure he stored every shot he hit as Good Enough, Good, or Great.

If we were forced to create a one-size-fits-all human-skills game plan (which we wouldn't), it would include these elements: Keep your Think Box simple and trust your intuition, or your gut brain. Be present in your body and access a sensory feel *before* you step into your Play Box. Keep your Play Box engaged and short. Be neutral and objective about your bad shots, and store your best shots in your Memory Box. Keep your body language strong, and focus your energy on something positive; stay mentally in the present, rather than thinking about the past or the future.

After your round is the time for evaluation. Again, most players look at their scores and statistics, and make their evaluations based on them. We urge you to evaluate how you did with your human-skills game plan first. It is your human skills *and* your process that produced the statistics. Evaluating process first will also improve your positivity bias and your storage of memories. How committed did you stay to your decisions and your playing focus? The more attention you pay to these skills (again, the only ones under your control), the more your outcomes will improve.

Here are three simple questions to ask yourself after each round: What did I do that was really good? What do I want to do better? How will I accomplish it? It could be that you noticed you lost your balance on a number of swings, so you'll put extra practice into balance. You might've been confused about your decision-making on several occasions, so you'll work on being clear on your decisions, then committing fully to them. It could be technical: "I'm not sure how to hit a high bunker shot, and I want to learn."

AFTER A ROUND:

- How did you do with your playing focus?

YOUR CONTROLLABLE GOAL

- 3 Questions
  - WHAT WAS GOOD?
  - WHAT CAN BE BETTER?
  - HOW ARE YOU GOING TO DO IT? ACTION!
- Other stats
  - GREENS HIT
  - FAIRWAYS HIT
  - PUTTS
  - UPS & DOWNS

After winning the U.S. Women's Open in 2016, Brittany Lang began making her game plan for the Women's British Open just a few weeks later. "My particular playing foci were alignment and keeping my head down during putts," she explained. "But my real game plan is always my process, committing to my decisions, being present to my shots, and creating DHEA by being happy. These are the skills I've been working on for years. It's easy to make them my game plan."

YOUR HUMAN-SKILLS GAME PLAN

WE PROMISE that creating a solid human-skills game plan will change your game forever. Whatever particulars you decide on, these are our VISION54 truths:

• Every golfer will improve by fully committing to their decisions.

• Every golfer will play better by being more present in the Play Box.

• Every golfer will play better if they react objectively to their bad shots, and positively store their good shots in their Memory Box.

HUMAN-SKILLS GAME PLAN: QUESTIONS

• What's most important for you to do in your Think Box?

• What's most important for you to do during your shot in the Play Box?

• What's most important for you to do in the Memory Box?

• What's most important for you to do between shots to recharge and access your best physical, mental, emotional states?

• What are the ingredients of your MY54—what is unique about your best golf?

• What are the main ingredients of your NOT54—how do you get in your own way?

• What are your best tools to shift from NOT54 to MY54?

• What's most important for you to pay attention to during a round that is under your control—your one, main playing focus?

HUMAN-SKILLS GAME PLAN WARM-UP

• How are you feeling today?

• What's most important for you to do in preparation for a round?

- What's your best way to warm up your swing and create good physical, mental, and emotional states before playing?
- If you get to the course late or get stressed out by something outside your game, what will your emergency warm-up be?

HUMAN-SKILLS GAME PLAN: ON-COURSE EXPLORATIONS

CREATE A GAME PLAN for nine holes. Decide on one to three things to focus on that are under your control during the entire nine holes, and rate yourself on how well you paid attention to them. Make a "playing focus" scorecard, and rate yourself on a scale of 1 to 5 (5 being best) about how well you committed to each playing focus.

The following explorations represent a "mastery" game plan for human skills. We're presenting it not because we expect that you'll be able to achieve it right away, but because it's interesting to consider. Michael Murphy's friend and colleague George Leonard wrote a book, *Mastery*, that explains "the mysterious process during which what is at first difficult becomes progressively easier and more pleasurable through practice." He also writes that mastery "is not really a goal or a destination, but rather a process, a journey." We hope you'll engage these explorations in this spirit. Eventually, you can evaluate yourself on these criteria over 18 holes.

1. Play Box: For nine holes, I was 100-percent committed to every shot in my Play Box.

2. Think Box: For nine holes, I was 100-percent committed to my decision for every shot.

3. Memory Box: For nine holes, I was either objective/neutral or positive/happy for each of my post-shot reactions. My criterion for being happy about a shot is when it's Good Enough, Good, or Great.

4. Balance: For nine holes, I finished in balance on every shot.

5. Tempo: For nine holes, I was keenly aware of my tempo and adjusted it as needed.

6. Tension Awareness: For nine holes, I was aware of the tension levels in my body, and I adjusted them when necessary.

7. Resilience: For nine holes, I effectively managed my adrenaline levels. I came off the golf course with more energy, more DHEA, and feeling better about myself than when I began the round—no matter the outcome.

8. Self-Talk: For nine holes, I managed my self-talk and was able to quiet my mind as needed.

9. Master of Variability: For nine holes, I caught myself when one of my NOT54 tendencies appeared, and I started shifting immediately to MY54.

HUMAN-SKILLS GAME PLAN EVALUATION

- What was Good Enough, Good, or Great about your game today? (Give a minimum of three things.)
- What could have been better (start with the most important "better")?
- What actions will you take to bring about these changes?

PIA: THE INTEGRAL KEN WILBER

WE FIRST HEARD about Ken Wilber through Michael Murphy. He was a young philosopher and scholar who had hung out at Esalen for a while before moving to Colorado. Wilber ran a website that was kind of an underground hangout. You wouldn't have known about it unless someone told you. He conducted interviews called "Ken Wilber Dialogues" with artists, writers, and thinkers. We downloaded them, listened to some of them, and were totally inspired.

Wilber had been a pre-med student at Duke University in the late 1960s before he became interested in Eastern thought and history. He also took deep dives into psychology, history, culture, physics, you name it. After two years of college, he dropped out, as he said, "to sit in a room by myself and stare at a wall for five years."

I read Wilber's book called *The Theory of Everything*. He's an amazing synthesizer of the world's most important ideas, histories, and philosophies. He's fluent in science, art, and ethics, as well as physics, biology, aesthetics, and sociology. He reflects on politics, medicine, business, and even sports. Reading Wilber's book helped me look at the bigger picture. If Ken Wilber could connect the dots between just about everything that's ever happened in the history of the world, and help point us in a positive direction, how might we try to do the same in our world of golf?

Wilber says it doesn't make sense to point fingers at who is right and who is wrong. Instead, he suggests we look at the great things that people have done through history, look at the common denominators of good, and see how we can integrate all the best ideas to create something functional that helps people.

Wilber came up with a concept he calls Integral Theory, in which all human knowledge and experience are placed in a four-quadrant grid. The quadrants are: Individual-Interior (our thoughts, feelings, values, motivations, and state of consciousness); Individual-Exterior (our physical bodies, biology, neurology, and biomechanics); Collective-Interior (the "we" perspective, including values, language, mutual understanding, and relationships); and Collective-Exterior (the "it" perspective—social rules, environment, and people). The quadrants are part of a bigger, more holistic system with the acronym AQAL: All quadrants, all states, all lines, all levels, and all types of human experience.

Everything human beings do, including golf, can be seen through the frame of these quadrants. It was especially interesting to us because golf is such a first-person experience. No one can swing the club for you. No one can commit to decisions for you. No one can quell the nerves you feel standing over an important shot. That's why awareness is so critical. Unless you have a good understanding of yourself and your physical, mental, and emotional states, you're not going to be able to fully manage or access your capabilities. What intrigued us was how Wilber's framework could be relevant for golfers.

When Lynn and I get interested in something, we apply it first to our own lives and golf games to see how it works. We read another of Wilber's books, *Integral Life Practice*, which made his system more applicable. Wilber's model includes what he calls "Lines and Levels of Development." Everyone has core capabilities, including cognitive, physical, and emotional, which we can choose to develop over our lifetimes. How much we choose to develop is up to us.

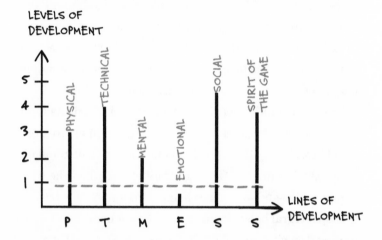

As human beings, we have an exterior world and an interior world. If you're going to be great at something, you need to have good access to both. When you apply this filter to golf, you see that a great deal of effort has been expended on developing the exterior of the individual and the game: fitness, technique, and equipment. Golfers' technical skills are fairly advanced, relatively speaking, because that's where they've put most of their energy. At VISION54, we're trying to add the interior piece for those who are interested. We believe that people can become better, more well-rounded golfers if they have a baseline of both exterior and interior skills.

I wanted to see how I could beef up my own integral life practices. Basically, if we agree that life is multidimensional, and that golf is multidimensional, I can choose to focus on a number of things: developing my physical body, developing aspects of my mind, working on how I react emotionally, and how I interact with others, even improving my willpower, ethics, and spiritual life. All of these will help me become a better golfer (and person). The trick is to not get stuck thinking that if I devote myself to one or two things—fitness and technique, for example—I will reach my full potential. Each of us needs to figure out which particular human skills will most strengthen our games. Then we need to practice them.

I made a multidimensional plan. I worked out daily on my fitness; then I read a book for 30 minutes in an area that would broaden my thinking. I meditated twice a day, and did a few extra minutes of "feeling" gratitude. If I had the time, I'd take a hike and experience being in nature. The point is to develop integral habits in life that keep your body, mind, emotions, and spirit awake. If you apply the system to golf, it might mean that I would check my posture or ball position regularly, but also practice meditation and focus exercises to improve my ability to stay in the present in my Play Box. If I had time, I would do the practices for longer durations. If I was busy, I'd do some of them for 10 minutes, or five minutes—even one minute, if necessary.

I practice these things today. It's important to keep them up. The mistake some of our golfers make is when they start to work on inner skills and find themselves playing better, but after some time, they think they've done enough—and so they fall back to working only on their technique. Or they think because they've learned a few inner skills, their work stops there.

We need to be both flexible and disciplined in creating and sustaining new habits. The point is that these skills are foundational—keep practicing them!

Wilber (and Michael Murphy) believe that only an integral approach to the body, mind, emotions, heart, and spirit can truly create access to your full capacities, and thus the "flow" or "zone" or peak-performance state. Wilber says these performance states are the equivalent of altered or non-ordinary states of consciousness and have parallels in the world's great meditative and contemplative systems. In short, spiritual experiences can occur in sports.

Most of our VISION54 skills are human skills aimed at drawing out the interior capacities of the individual. Wilber's ideas helped us come up with our own VISION54 acronym for the elements we feel are important to how we play golf: PTMESS stands for Physical, Technical, Mental, Emotional, Social, and Spirit of the Game.

One particular Wilber quote continues to resonate with us on and off the course, because it's truly what we believe: "Every area of life is a place to practice and to develop as human beings."

CHAPTER **12**

BECOME A SUPERGOLFER:
GLIMPSES INTO THE FUTURE
OF PERFORMANCE

N THE EARLY 1950S, very few people believed a human being was capable of running a mile in under four minutes. Runners had been talking about the possibility since the mid-1700s, and trying to break the elusive barrier since the early 1900s. By the mid-1940s, the time for the mile had been lowered to 4 minutes, 1.01 seconds, where it stubbornly remained. Then, on May 6, 1954, a 25-year-old British man named Roger Bannister shattered the record, running the mile in 3 minutes, 59.4 seconds.

Bannister was Britain's best middle-distance runner. He had started his running career as a 17-year-old student at Oxford University, and competed in the 1500 meters at the 1952 Olympic Games in Helsinki, Finland. He first set his sights on the mile when he was a medical student in 1953. He devised a specialized training program that drew on both old and new training regimens. He studied the physiological challenge of running the mile, measuring his own oxygen consumption levels and writing papers with titles such as "The Carbon Dioxide Stimulus to Breathing in Severe Exercise." Through trial and error, he learned that running consistent lap times required less oxygen than varying his pace. Bannister researched the innovative training methods of Swedish milers Arne Andersson and Gunder Hägg. Hägg had set the record for the mile in 1945 (4 minutes, 1 second) using the Swedish "fartlek" method of training, in which high-intensity bursts of running were interspersed with slower-paced intervals or rest. Bannister adopted the method, focusing on quarter-mile splits. During his lunch hour, he would run 10 splits, punctuated by two-minute rests. At the end of five months, he lowered his split time from 63 seconds to 59 seconds.

Another method he employed in training was to close his eyes and "see" the running of a sub-four-minute mile over and over in his brain, to try to create the actual sensation in his body and his mind. A few years earlier, psychologists had begun to think about how their field might help athletes improve performance. They experimented with techniques such as progressive relaxation, positive affirmations, mental practices, and something they called visualization. Bannister chose to practice visualization.

The race he selected for his record-breaking attempt on the mile was a meet between Oxford University and the [British] Amateur Athletic Association. Bannister took the train from London to Oxford on a spring day in May. Two of his former Oxford teammates, Chris Chataway and Chris Brasher, had agreed to be "rabbits," or pacemakers. Later, Bannister recalled, "As the gun fired, Chris Chataway went into the lead, and I slipped effortlessly in behind him, feeling tremendously full of running. My legs seemed to meet no resistance at all, almost as if impelled by an unknown force. We seemed to be going so slowly. Impatiently, I shouted, 'Faster!'"

The conditions were ideal. A brisk wind had dropped to nothing as the race began. At one-and-a-half laps, Bannister was still worrying that the pace wasn't fast enough. His coach shouted from the crowd, "Relax!"

"I obeyed," he said later. "It was too late to do anything about it, so why worry?"

Bannister barely noticed the half-mile mark passing by at 1 minute, 58 seconds. He was on pace. "I was relaxing so much that my mind seemed almost detached from my body," he recalled. "It was incredible that we could run at this speed without strain." At this point, Chris Brasher took over as the rabbit.

At the three-quarter-mile mark, Bannister was still running with ease. He knew a four-minute mile was possible. With 300 yards remaining, he surged past Brasher. "I felt the moment of a lifetime had come," he said. The remaining few seconds before he hit the finish line tape seemed to go on forever. "I leapt at it like a man taking his last spring to save himself from a chasm that threatens to engulf him. My effort was over, my collapse almost unconscious. . . . It was only then that the real pain overtook me. I knew I had done it before anyone even said the words."

Bannister's 3-minute, 59.4-second mile seemed to instantly dissolve the imaginative, mental, and physical barriers that had kept other runners from breaking the record. Forty-six days later, after years of trying, an Australian runner named John Landy lowered Bannister's record to 3 minutes, 58 seconds. The following year, three runners broke four minutes; the next year five runners did it. Today, more than 4,000 male runners have broken four minutes; the current record of 3 minutes, 43.13 seconds was set by Moroccan Hicham El Gerrouj in 1999.

We love the story of Roger Bannister for a couple of reasons. First, he set a goal for himself that had never been achieved.

Second, he formulated a training plan that involved both traditional and innovative, untested strategies. He created his own VISION 3:59.

Kjell Enhager was the person who first came up with the goal of 54 for golfers. As we've mentioned, he had joined Pia and the other coaches who were working with the elite Swedish golfers in the early 1990s. The young golfers kept making excuses about why they would never be great on the world stage. The coaches were determined to change their mind-sets. Kjell noted that most of the players had made birdies on each of the holes at their home courses. What would it take for them to birdie every hole and shoot 54, the equivalent of a perfect round?

Like a four-minute mile, 54 is a number that serves as a goal, but it's also a metaphor, a philosophy, and an approach to golf at every level. For us, 54 is an attitude that accentuates the possibilities of our abilities. It's also a process: What will you choose to focus on that you can fully manage during a round? It's a discipline: What will you do to make this a real-life practice and not just a concept? Finally, we see 54 as an aspiration. We often see increased levels of commitment and performance when players have a purpose higher than themselves, when they're inspired by a specific goal or person or event.

With nods to Kjell Enhager (who coined the term *superfluid*), Michael Murphy (who came up with the idea of supernormal), and Ken Wilber (who conceived the concept of a Superhuman Operating System), we call the future player who will shoot 54 in competition the Supergolfer. The Supergolfer will be someone who will clearly commit to a decision in the Think Box. The Supergolfer will be able to create a deep and engaged Play Box for every shot during a round, shifting from a left-brain analytic state to a right-brain performance state with ease. The Supergolfer will be able to adapt to internal and external variabilities on the course as they arise. The Supergolfer will manage Memory Boxes and emotions. The Supergolfer will manage the state of his or her physical body, creating DHEA and limiting cortisol at will. The Supergolfer will manage self-talk; the Supergolfer will recognize NOT54s as soon as they appear, and shift seamlessly to MY54s. The Supergolfer will master the intricacies of swing technique, fitness, and equipment—and also foundational human skills.

In the Supergolfer's round of 54, there won't be perfect conditions, a perfect warm-up, or a perfect swing. Expecting perfection is unrealistic. In the future, golfers will begin to learn human skills on the same day they learn to grip a golf club. Human skills aren't merely "add-ons" or "mental" skills. They are fundamental skills that will help carry every individual golfer to a new performance threshold.

Every Supergolfer will be unique. Among the players we've worked with at VISION54 over the years are eight golfers who have won major championships, as well as players who have won tournaments on every professional tour. They range from tall to short, introverted to extroverted, and religious to non-religious. They are long and not-so-long hitters. Each one has the potential to become the first Supergolfer, but like Roger Bannister, he or she must put together the right ingredients. For one player, it might land on mental or emotional discipline; for another, it might be finding a way to be more physically present, to commit even more deeply to each shot. And for another player, it might be achieving perfect overall control of their game.

$$P + T + M + E + S + S = 54$$

PHYSICAL TECHNICAL MENTAL EMOTIONAL SOCIAL SPIRIT OF
THE GAME

Among the players we have worked with and influenced, Annika Sorenstam is the one we think has come closest to actualizing and integrating the elements of *being a player*: the physical, technical, mental, emotional, social, and spiritual components of the game. That is, she is the player who has come closest to being a Supergolfer. Not coincidentally, she is one of the nearly 20 players (and the only woman) to have shot 59 in competition. (Jim Furyk broke the 59 barrier when he shot a 58 at the Travelers Championship in 2016.)

Annika shot 59 in March 2001, during the second round of the Standard Register Ping Tournament in Phoenix. "I remember how I felt," she recalls. "The day started normally. I had my routine, and everything was fine. I birdied the first six holes, but I had done that before, so I didn't overreact. It was when I got to the 7th hole that I started realizing what I was doing. When you figure out that you're 7 under par after 7 holes, you go, *Wow, I've never done this before.*

"I went to the 8th tee. A part of me was really excited, but another part of me started to feel nervous, like I needed to protect it. I was going back and forth in my head. I said to myself, *This is what you always believed you could do. This is the way you visualized it. Now it's happening. Don't be afraid.*

"Mentally, I was able to push away my distractions and anxiety. *Take the chance, Annika. It's here. Golf may be serious, but it's still just a game.* I knew I couldn't stand over my shots too long or think too much. I was trying to be proud and strong and confident. If I could maintain my confidence on the outside, maybe it would bleed into my insides."

Annika birdied hole No. 8 for her eighth consecutive birdie. Then she made par on the No. 9 hole. "It was almost a relief, because I was in danger of getting distracted by outcome," she says. "I told myself that I needed to get back to committing to each shot, and let everything else come."

Annika made four straight birdies after the turn; she was 12-under after 13 holes. At the finish, her round of 59 included 13 birdies, five pars, and 25 putts on a 6,459-yard course. She missed one fairway, and reached every green in regulation. "I had thought about it for so long, and in the end, I was able to conquer it," she says. "Yes, I left a few shots out there, but I didn't leave them out there because I didn't commit. Every shot felt good. Right after the round I told Pia, 'Now I know it's even more possible to shoot 54.'"

Rodney Yee is one of the most famous yogis in the world. We know him through a mutual friend, and we love his perspective on human performance and breaking barriers. "I was a dancer before I was a yogi," Rodney says. "I've experienced peak performance, or 'the zone' or 'flow,' whatever you want to call the state. When I was in it, my natural perceptions shifted, and I began to see and feel something that I normally didn't experience and perceive. I felt coordinated in a completely different way. It really does feel like a coming together, like you're in a river and you're swimming with the current or accessing some other energy. It's the perfect confluence, and the conditions feel like they're thrusting you toward your goal, rather than you using a lot of effort to reach it."

What are these energies and conditions? We don't yet fully know scientifically, but different cultures have held different theories about them. Rodney says: "In yoga, the primal energy that lies coiled at the base of the spine is called the Kundalini. It's usually represented in art as a goddess or a serpent waiting to be awakened. The awakening, whether through the postures of yoga, breathing, meditation, running, or playing golf, involves the Kundalini moving up the central channel of the body to reach the chakra at the top of the head. Some yogis describe the feeling as an electric current running up the spine. The question is, do we control the Kundalini? Or do we control the conditions so that when it begins to awaken, we're able to get out of our own way and into its flow? When Kundalini rises, time slows down, and your perceptions change. In this state, the golf hole might look huge, as if you couldn't miss it if you tried."

THE BEST GOLFERS in the world work extremely hard on their swing techniques. They work on their fitness. They have clubs perfectly fitted to their techniques and their bodies. But these might not be sufficient ingredients for golfers to reach a new performance threshold. Roger Bannister failed several times before he broke the mile record. He needed to find new, out-of-the-box methods to add to his traditional regimens. Eventually, he adopted the new technique of visualization. He kept sensitizing his body and mind to the different inputs and feelings he would need to accomplish something nobody had ever before accomplished. In sports, the body is the tool. But it isn't just the physical body or the mental body. A highly complex and integral human being is involved. Rodney says that preparation at this level of athletic endeavor is akin to sharpening the blade of a knife. "When you sharpen something to an extreme level, every little angle of the blade counts. If you sharpen part of the blade too much, you'll dull it. In performance, for instance, you may sharpen your attention to the point where it's really, really fine. But the sharper it gets, the more every little thing will affect it, because now you're getting to a molecular level. If your emotions didn't count so much before, they count now. If your feelings about your girlfriend didn't come into play before, they may now. That favorite sweater that makes you feel lucky because you're superstitious—that counts even more now."

In 2006, Arron Oberholser came heartbreakingly close to shooting 59—to his own knife edge of perfection. In falling short, he shed more light on what might be required than some of the players who have succeeded. We'll let Arron tell his story:

"I was playing in the Byron Nelson tournament," he recalls. "I remember I got to Dallas and shot 74 in the first round. I called my girlfriend at the time—now my wife. She said, 'How did you play?' I said, 'Terrible. I'm going to need to shoot 60 or 59 tomorrow just to make the cut.'

"The next day I get started, and I make a couple of putts, and everything is going well. I can't remember whether it was the 4th or 5th hole, but I drained a putt from about 30 feet. It went over a rise, navigated two breaks, and rolled right into the heart of the hole. I'm like, *Wow. I guess the putter is working today.*

"I kept going, hitting good shot after good shot, and making putts. All of a sudden, I'm 7-under after 12 holes. After 15 holes, I'm 8-under with three holes to play. We walk to No. 16 hole, which most guys can reach with an iron on their second shot.

"I knew I had a chance to shoot 59 if I could birdie the last three holes, or make an eagle and two birdies. It was totally do-able. I looked at my caddie and said, 'Hey, if I birdie the last three, I shoot 59.' I knew I needed to break the tension. I stripe a drive, then hit a 4-iron just short in the bunker. I blast an easy shot out to 6 inches, and make the putt. Birdie.

"I wasn't nervous. I was having fun. I was embracing it. I had an opportunity to do something that had only been done four times in history at that point. I was going to be the fifth guy to shoot 59 on the PGA Tour. I birdied No. 17 hole.

"I get to the 18th tee, and I superstitiously say the same thing to my caddie. 'Hey, if I birdie No. 18 hole, I shoot 59.' At this point he's not smiling anymore. He's nervous. I get over the ball and put the peg in the ground. It's not a driver hole, so I have a 3-wood in my hands. Now I'm totally immersed in what I'm doing—I'm super aware of my surroundings—my awareness level is sky high.

"Suddenly, from 250 or 300 yards away, I hear a gas-powered maintenance cart coming up the path. I'm literally in my Play Box over the ball, and the red light in my brain starts going off. *Don't hit the ball, Arron! Don't hit! Don't hit!*

"I step out of my Play Box. I gather myself. Then I step back in. My nerves kick in. All of a sudden, I'm not having fun anymore. Just like that, a gas-powered cart gets into my head, and I can't get the feeling back—the feeling of heightened awareness, of well-being, and having a great time in the zone. I couldn't get it back.

"I popped up my tee shot. Luckily it landed in the fairway on the top of the hill. I recovered enough to hit one of the best 3-irons I've ever hit. The ball was on the green. I'd left myself a 15-foot putt for 59.

"When I walk onto the green, my hands are shaking. I'm feeling like there isn't enough time in the world for me to gather myself to make the stroke I know I'm capable of making. There was nothing in me that was present anymore in my Play Box during that putt. The minute I hit it, I knew it wasn't going in."

Arron says, "In retrospect, it wasn't just the cart that broke my concentration. I couldn't stop myself from thinking about the outcome. *Wow, I can be the fifth guy to shoot 59.* I couldn't stop thinking about the history, and the adulation I was about to receive.

"I couldn't get out of my own way."

Arron finished the round with two-putt and a 60. "There's the present, and there's nothing else," he says. "The big question under extreme pressure is, how do you do it? What tools do you need to get yourself there?"

To reach every new goal, to surpass each new barrier, a player needs to find the right ingredients, and the precise way to sharpen the knife. After Ariya Jutanugarn's three-hole collapse in the final round of the 2016 ANA Inspiration, we worked with her to develop a deeper and stronger Play Box that would function under intense pressure. The new Play Box was the sharpened knife; she won the next three tournaments, and became the first player in LPGA Tour history to record the first three wins of her career in consecutive tournaments.

Four months later, Ariya set her sights on winning her first major. In July, she arrived at Woburn Country Club, north of

London, for the Ricoh Women's British Open. During the first two rounds, she shot 65 and 69. In the third round, she made six birdies and 12 pars to shoot 66. That evening, she told us that despite her score, she didn't feel she was committing fully or deeply enough in her Play Box. We knew that with the pressure of leading a major on the final day, she would be even more stressed.

We talked it over. Ariya knew she would need to take more deep breaths with longer exhales during the round to manage her adrenaline. She would need to monitor the tension in her upper body. She would need to commit to stronger Play Box "feelings" of joy and happiness. She went into her round with a clear game plan and playing focus. Even when she double-bogeyed the 13th hole and her six-shot lead shrank to one shot, she didn't lose her focus. Ariya birdied No. 17, and went on to win her first major championship.

One month later, she won the Canadian Pacific Women's Open. In November, she tied for 4th place in the CME Group Tour Championship, clinching the 2016 Rolex Player of the Year Award. In addition to her five victories during the season, she had 10 top-10 finishes in 28 starts. And that wasn't all. In 2016, Ariya set a new LPGA record for most birdies in a single season with 469, shattering Stacy Lewis's 2014 record by 18 birdies. Finally, she won the LPGA money title and CME Globe title, earning a season-ending $1 million bonus.

The player we met early in the year was ranked 64th in the world, and had been afraid to hit the golf ball the season before. She had melted down while leading the final holes of the ANA Inspiration tournament shortly after we began working with her. But over the course of her season, Ariya strengthened and deepened her command of her new human skills.

She ended the 2016 season ranked No. 2 in the Rolex Women's World Golf Rankings.

Rodney Yee says there is a connection between technique and freedom—one informs the other; neither succeeds alone. We know that the best golfers in the world possess expert technique. We believe that human skills can open the door to freedom.

We want to acknowledge a conundrum here. Breakthrough performances and reaching never-achieved goals can be an almost impossible trap. How do we humans get beyond pressure, expectations, and the admiration that accompanies great talent and success? "That's why these performers are heroes," says Rodney. "People don't become great golf champions or great musicians only because of talent—they become champions because they can withstand all the other stuff that gets thrown at them, and still find the sharp edge of focus.

"Yo-Yo Ma may not be the best cellist in the world," he says, "but he has an ability to play at an extraordinarily high level with great consistency. Where's his eye looking in order to endure (and ignore) these other things called fame and fortune? He can summon a level of 'ordinary.' When he gets on the biggest stage, he can make the switch. He's just a regular guy then, kind of like the Dalai Lama. He's like, 'I'm just playing the cello. I'm just playing a concert.' When he's on the biggest stage in the world, he can de-escalate the importance, and the pressure."

Arron Oberholser understood this, even as he fell agonizingly short of shooting 59. "You have to walk that knife edge to reach peak performance," he says. "On one side, it's caring too much. On the other side, it's not caring enough. If you can navigate the edge, that's where 'the zone' is. That's what having fun looks like. When you care too much, you don't perform. When you care too little, you don't perform. You have to tell yourself, *I don't care if I miss this putt. I don't care if I hit this 4-iron in the water.* Because I love where I am and what I'm doing."

That human skill is the ability to find a deeper detachment—in other words, a new level of being present.

One final skill the Supergolfer will need is the ability to manage her or his story. The difference between shooting 54 and not shooting 54 might very well be the story we tell ourselves. Can we free ourselves to be as good as we can be and enable our authentic greatness to emerge without the whisper of fear, anxiety, or negativity? Ken Wilber says: "The battle with the self is the battle you must fight and win if you intend to perform to your full potential. Any competition with your opponent is secondary. The primary competition is fought within you: the inner battle, the inner struggle, the inner game."

One of our favorite students, Janet Daniels of Arizona, has improved greatly using her VISION54 human skills, going from a 19-handicap to a 12-handicap over the last several years. At the end of one VISION54 program, she shared with us that her mother, also a fine golfer, had been "ladylike" and intentionally non-aggressive on the golf course. "Honestly it was never important to her to win, and she kind of pushed that on me—don't stand out, don't be the star, you're not a princess. I'm sure I internalized those messages, because I never pushed myself. I thought being a 19-handicap golfer was just fine."

Lynn told Janet, "We think you need to give yourself permission to go low. We think you need to give yourself permission to be a *really* good player. And we think you need to give yourself permission to rewrite your own story. "

At 55 years old, that's what Janet is now doing. "I've given myself permission to be the one out there to go low," she says. "I never thought it was my place, or my turn, but now I do."

Thinking about peak performance has led us to the idea of the sublime. The definition of the word is "of such excellence, grandeur, or beauty as to inspire great admiration or awe." Interestingly, *sublime* is a verb as well as a noun. It's related to chemistry; it's the process in which a solid substance changes into vapor when heated, then returns to solid form as it cools. The word *sublime* suggests an ineffable experience—looking at a sunset, appreciating a painting, listening to a piece of music, or tasting something exquisitely delicious. The sublime is something that carries us to a meditative state that approaches the deepest satisfaction and joy.

We believe VISION54's human skills offer every player the possibility of experiencing the sublime in his or her game. We believe everyone can break through barriers to achieve their true potential. We believe human skills will give you tools you've never possessed before. Your human skills, as you explore them, will continue to be yours, always under your control. Put as much fortitude, discipline, and commitment into developing your human skills as you do your technique and your fitness, and you may very well become the Supergolfer of the future.

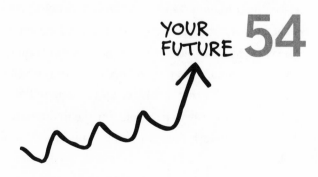

BECALMING A BETTER
AND HAPPIER GOLFER

WE USE SUPERGOLFER as an analogy about where human skills can take us—in golf and in life. What we're equally interested in is better and happier golfers at every level. We know we'll continue to learn more about the science of human performance. Equipment and technology will continue to evolve. But as long as we're playing the game of golf, we'll need human skills to help us decide on a shot, commit to our decisions, stay present and sensory-based while performing, and manage our emotions. We'll need human skills to be players.

Every year, we spend part of the summer in Torekov, a beautiful village on Sweden's southwest coast. In 2016, we did a day of on-course coaching with the members of the Torekov Golf Club. Seventy-two players went out on a rainy day for an 18-hole shotgun. They carried their own bags or used push carts. We said to them, "You're not here to score, so you don't have to hole out. We just want you to do the following explorations."

They explored. They experimented. They practiced internal and external awareness. Some things worked right away. Others didn't. We told them they would need time and courage to fully explore their human skills.

Over the next few days, members came up to us at the club and in the village. Some told us the four hours went by quicker than any other round. Others said they were amazed at the engagement and focus they'd achieved. One lady told us, "I feel that I have a new way to play golf. For the first time ever, I didn't focus on my technique and score, but on my human skills. I played so much better!"

So pick up a club. Go out onto the course and explore your human skills. Have fun. Find the ones that work for you, develop them, and take ownership of them. They could be the keys to your best golf—and your best life.

ON-COURSE EXPLORATIONS:
18 HOLES FOR BETTER AND HAPPIER GOLF

HERE ARE THE 18-HOLE, on-course explorations we gave to our friends in Torekov. Practice one on each hole. Your intention is to:

• Be more aware of your performance state.

• Discover how well you keep attention on your performance state instead of on outcome and technique.

• Discover what helps you play better and enjoy the game more.

After each hole, rate yourself on a scale of 1–5 (5 being the best) on how well you kept your attention on the task. After six, 12, and 18 holes, write down which explorations helped you enjoy the game more or made you play better.

You do not need to score. You can move your ball from lies you don't like on the fairways and greens. This is a true "training and exploring" round.

HOLE 1: Feel soft, relaxed shoulders during each of your swings.

HOLE 2: On each shot, feel 50-percent tempo during the entire swing.

HOLE 3: Hum during your swing on each shot.

HOLE 4: Hit all your full shots with your feet together; putt on one leg (right or left); finish each shot in balance.

HOLE 5: Experience a strong lower-body "feel" during the setup to your swing; feel extra-strong body language between shots.

HOLE 6: See the target or the ball flight or the line of the putt in your mind's eye before each shot. Assign it your favorite color during the entire swing.

Which one of these made you play better or enjoy your golf more?

HOLE 7: Close your eyes and feel your commitment for five seconds before stepping into each shot.

HOLE 8: Say something authentically positive about the process or outcome of each shot.

HOLE 9: Go from feeling free to "freer" as you finish each swing.

HOLE 10: Play this hole as a silent hole. Don't talk to yourself or others. See, feel, listen, and smell everything around you!

HOLE 11: Count or sing during each of your swings.

HOLE 12: Feel 60-percent tempo in each backswing and 80-percent tempo in each forward swing.

Which one of these made you play better or enjoy your golf more?

HOLE 13: Say your decision about each shot aloud with a confident voice and strong body language.

HOLE 14: Feel constant grip pressure during each swing.

HOLE 15: Take breaths with long exhales before each shot, and feel a sense of joy when you swing the club.

HOLE 16: Play this as an "instinct" hole. Do not check the yardage, think about the shot, or take practice swings. Listen to your gut, and hit each shot with pure feel.

HOLE 17: Keep your mouth slightly open during each of your swings, and imagine the sight and sound of the ocean between shots.

HOLE 18: Hold your finish for three seconds after the completion of each shot. Feel deep happiness for your Good Enough, Good, and Great shots.

Which one of these made you play better or enjoy your golf more?

ACKNOWLEDGMENTS

"Make the implicit explicit."

Those are the words that Michael Murphy—founder of the Esalen Institute, author of *Golf in the Kingdom*, and now a treasured friend—said to us in 2001 when he joined us at one of our coaching seminars.

Michael has long believed, as have we, that golfers will never achieve their best performances by practicing technique alone. He also believes that most people use only a fraction of their human capacities, and he challenged us to create an environment where golfers could learn about—and access—their full human potential. In challenging us to make the implicit skills of the great champions, and of peak performance, explicit, Michael gave us our most ambitious assignment.

In *Be a Player*, we've made the "human skills" we believe are necessary for great golf explicit. So our first acknowledgment, and profound thanks, go to Michael Murphy.

We want to thank our small but powerful VISION54 team in Scottsdale, Arizona. We wouldn't be able to do this work as effectively without Kristine Reese, Tiffany Yager, Zach Theut, and Lisa Elliott, who are passionately motivated every day to support golfers of all levels to improve their performance *on the course* and to enjoy the game more.

We want to thank the hundreds of players who have sailed into our VISION54 harbor over the years, as well as all the golf teachers who have attended our 54COACH trainings. Whatever level of golfer, you continue to teach us, motivate us, and inspire us each and every day.

Be a Player started as a series of conversations with veteran golf writer and *Sports Illustrated* contributor John Garrity, who helped us tease the explicit out of the implicit. Our cowriter, Susan Reed, continued those conversations and created this book with us. We first met Susan in 2002 when she was editor of *Golf for Women* magazine. Ever since, through our many talks about life and the game, Susan has been an integral part of our VISION54 journey. We are beyond grateful for Susan's friendship, humor, work ethic, and creativity. She always asks the right questions at the right time and challenges us to think more deeply and clearly.

This is our first book with Atria Books, part of Simon & Schuster. We want to thank Atria's visionary publisher, Judith Curr (also a golfer), for saying yes to this project, for understanding our mission, and for believing in it. Our brilliant editor, Rakesh Satyal, was incisive, steady, and drew out the best in us—and in this book. The Atria team was first-rate: copyeditor Stephen Hennessey, Deputy Director of Publicity David Brown, Editorial Assistant Loan Le, and designer Tim Oliver each contributed their incredible talents.

Thank you to our longtime agent, David McCormick, who has been with us for our last two books. That you are holding *Be a Player* in your hands is a tribute to his experience and professionalism.

We want to acknowledge the love of our friends and role models who were not explicitly part of this book. Many are like a second family: Annette Thompson, Pam Barnett, and Manuel de la Torre in particular have profoundly shaped our view of the game and taught us foundational life skills. Your professionalism and generosity live forever in our hearts.

We acknowledge (and are grateful for) the frustration that Pia felt as a young professional on the LPGA Tour when her skills didn't fully show up in competition. This conundrum and challenge was her greatest inspiration in exploring new ways of coaching and practicing.

We are thankful for the confusion Lynn felt as a relatively new golf teacher when her students came back to her with improved technique but asked, "Why aren't my scores going down?" or "Why am I playing worse?" This problem motivated Lynn to search out resources that would help her teach from a different paradigm.

We humbly acknowledge the courage it has required for us to take time away from teaching every year and commit to undisturbed "recharge time" in Torekov, Sweden. It has been invaluable for us to be in a place where we can be creative, think outside the box, and have time to listen to what our brains, hearts, and guts want to tell us. Torekov Golf Club is where we tested and tweaked many of the questions and explorations in the book.

Finally, we want to acknowledge each other—and our twenty-year creative partnership and collaboration. Synergy means 1+1 equals much more than 2. We started this journey believing in each other and our shared vision to influence the game for the better. We want to help golfers improve *on the course* and to enjoy the game more. We continue that pursuit every day with curiosity and an authentic commitment to the potential of the human spirit.

To our families in heaven and on this earth, thank you for your unconditional love and support.

ABOUT THE AUTHORS

PIA NILSSON and LYNN MARRIOTT have enjoyed extraordinary careers that have led them to international renown as the creators of the VISION54 program and the bestselling authors of three VISION54 books. Well known for their role in coaching Annika Sorenstam on her path to superstardom, Pia and Lynn have also fine-tuned the games of such notable students as LPGA Tour players Ariya Jutanugarn, Suzann Pettersen, Ai Miyazato, Brittany Lang, and Na Yeon Choi; PGA Tour players Kevin Streelman and Russell Knox; and amateurs such as former secretary of state and Augusta National Golf Club member Condoleezza Rice. Pia and Lynn are regularly included on *Golf Digest*'s annual list of 50 Best Teachers in America.

SUSAN K. REED is former editor-in-chief of *Golf for Women* magazine and a writer whose work has appeared in *Golf Digest*, *The New York Times Book Review*, *Travel & Leisure*, and other publications. She is the coauthor of the book *Yoga for Life: A Journey to Inner Peace and Freedom* with Colleen Saidman Yee. Susan lives in Sag Harbor, New York.

· · ·

For further information about VISION54, go to VISION54.com. There you will find our programs, trainings, and products to help you explore your game and build your human skills. You'll find the Online Learning Center, an area of the site that features digital downloads, learning sessions, interactive coaching exercises, and online self-evaluation tools. You'll also find a designated Be a Player *site where you can download a workbook to keep your game plan journal, as well as Playing Focus and MY54/NOT54 cards. And you can sign up for our VISION54 enews.*